YAEL HAFT-POMROCK

HANDS

Yael Haft-Pomrock

Hands

Aspects of Opposition and Complementarity in Archetypal Chirology

DAIMON
VERLAG

Yael Haft-Pomrock
Hands: Aspects of Opposition and Complementarity in Archetypal Chirology

ISBN 3-85630-536-X

Cover image: "Tingambato," a sculpture by Sergio Bustamante, photographed by Clint Clemens; cover design by Hanspeter 'James' Kälin.
Typesetting by r.a.i.

In memory and to the spirit of my son, Iron Wenderow
and my parents, Rivkah and Moshe Pomrock

For those who can wonder…
wonders appear.
The greatest wonder of all
is the human being.

Beneath your hands,
wonders will sprout.

Talking with Angels, p. 56

Contents

Foreword by Sylvia Brinton Perera

We know that our hands express and communicate as readily as they grasp and skillfully accomplish the tasks of life. They have many languages from signing for the deaf to forming mudras for the sacred dancer and priest. What we learn in this book and the works of other chirologists is that the very structure of our hands can tell us a great deal about our personality traits, inherited and learned patterns of reaction and behavior, and psychological dynamics and potentials. The forms of fingers and palm and lines reveal a language to help us to understand the psyche. The interpretation of the hand, which began as the ancient art of chiromancy, has been refined by recent and scientific studies of the hands of thousands of individuals. (A number of these have been done by Yael Haft herself.) These provide clear evidence that we can learn a great deal about a person through the careful and informed examination of his or her hands.

While therapists do not usually have the skill and opportunity to undertake the careful scrutiny using handprints as Yael Haft can do and as she here describes for us, we can nevertheless discover a great deal of useful information in an initial interview when we know something about chirology. After taking courses with Yael Haft, I have learned to pay attention to the hands of new clients as they tell me verbally why they have come for therapy. Along with their stories, dreams, general body language, and my own observations, their hands can illuminate basic personality characteristics. From even a cursory and unobtrusive perusal of the forms and expression of the backs of hands, the fingers, and thumb I have learned to get hints about ego-functioning, psychological qualities, potentials, and degree and kinds of pathology. I have come to appreciate that elementary chirology can be a useful tool for the practicing therapist.

For more detailed work I have had the advantage of being able to refer some clients to Mrs. Haft, who has since 1970 lectured in clinics and universities and given seminars on the feminine aspects – the goddess archetypes – in the hands. As a professional chirologist she is not only able to access the character of the clients in great depth, she can also tell me (when the client is willing to allow the communication) how the analysis is going and what childhood and current problems require greater attention. For the clients themselves such careful and accurate study of their hands can grant a view of their personality that feels as if it comes "from the mirror-eye of the Self," as one analysand said after her consultation. Such a picture of the whole personality is profoundly moving, for with an objectivity that feels numinous, it conveys the just-so reality of the person as he or she is at this time.

At a later time the hands will be different. They are remarkably responsive to changes in psyche, and a gifted chirologist like Yael Haft, will be able to observe and read the changes. While I have seen alterations in form, fingers, and lines over months and years, I could not have believed how precisely and quickly the hands express the sudden reactions in the psyche if I had not seen such a shift happen before my own eyes. In one class as we were practicing how to take handprints, one colleague had an intense emotional reaction in the moments between making her first and second left-hand print. We could easily see in the second handprint that a jagged sharpness in a line reaching out from her head line had registered the eruption of a complex and her defensive reaction. In a third print taken later the line had again softened.

While we are accustomed to reading emotions in the face, body postures, and armoring and while we are increasingly able to note the relevance of emotions to illness and of images to energic changes, it is not often that we are able to gain such a remarkable experience of the close and precise inter-functioning of body and psyche. Working with the tools of chirology we are forced to realize that body and psyche have indeed an interdependent existence. They are facets of one psychic-somatic whole. As Jung has said:

> "Mind and body are presumably a pair of opposites and, as such, the expression of a single entity whose essential nature is not knowable either from its outward, material manifestation or from inner, direct perception. According to an ancient belief, man arose from the coming together of a soul and a body. It would probably be more correct to speak of an unknowable living being, concerning the ultimate nature of which nothing can be said except that it vaguely expresses the quintessence of 'life.' This living being appears outwardly as the material body, but inwardly as a series of images of the vital activities taking place within it. They are two sides of the same coin…" (CW, Vol. 8, para. 619).

As therapists and students of the psyche, we need continually to expand our capacities to appreciate the multiple facets of this psychic-somatic whole, for it may be explored from many vantages. We can use dreams, chirology, transference and countertransference dynamics, bioenergetic assessments, active imaginations, and many other tools to gain access to the ultimately unknowable living being. All of these require practice. All of them require the capacities of the artist and the scientist. The subtle art of the chirologist is as remarkable and difficult as that of the dream interpreter. While dreams reveal their view of life-processes in images, the hand speaks in forms, lines, tonus, and other sensate expressions of bodily reality.

Although this book covers a difficult subject, requiring repeated perusal and detailed attentiveness, it introduces us to the embodied manifestations of psyche in the hand and teaches us some of the vocabulary with which we can become conscious of these. We are guided by a gifted chirologist who is also a therapist. She writes to share some of the tools of her trade, and she gives us actual photographs of many hands from her long practice to make our learning vivid. Thus she helps us to experience the mystery of the ultimately "unknowable living being" as it imprints itself in the hand. Unique among other books in this field is the intuitive-feeling approach and Yael Haft's use of archetypal images from Greek mythology–particularly those of the female deities. These images provide metaphors to illuminate the complex psychological meanings embodied in various areas of the hand. They help us to appreciate the subtle weaving together of collective imaginal symbols, psychological functioning, and bodily expression. These express our individual patterns of wholeness as aspects of the ultimately unknowable "quintessence of 'life.'"

Acknowledgments

My first thanks go to all my patients, clients and pupils, from whom I learned the most. I feel this is the proper occasion to thank all those who helped and supported me on my way: my teachers, collaborators and friends, Dr. Gusti Dreifuss, who opened to me the world of C.G. Jung and my becoming a chirologist and a therapist; Katya Klopfer, my main teacher and initiator in chirology, who was a pupil of Julius Spier: she has been my unfailing support and friend throughout my adult life, who has stood by me at all times; the late Dr. Hugo Debrunner, with whom I studied in Switzerland in 1964, corroborating many of his findings within my work, Dr. Morton Kaufman and Dr. Liliane Frey-Rohn. I am grateful for the two meetings I have had with Dr. Marie-Louise von Franz. They are unforgettable and they sustained me for a long time.

Prof. Pierre Soliman, who back in 1968 was Chief Psychologist of the Government Mental Hospital in Acre, became interested in my work. We compared the usual battery of projective tests and the chirology test. It was a pilot research of only nine patients. Once we had agreed on a common psychoanalytic (Freudian versus Jungian) terminology, the results coincided. Some of the things seen in the chirological test did not appear in the projective tests but did appear later in the psychotherapy of the patients. A year later, we did another chirological test describing what had happened and in which ways there have been improvements, regressions or deterioration. My findings were confirmed by the therapists. This research was never published but a wholesome friendship ensued.

My acknowledgment goes to Dr. Yigal Ginat, Chief Director of the Government Mental Hospital Talbieh, in Jerusalem, with whom I performed a research as to the differences between schizophrenic and normal controls using chirological (hand) testing, which was published. It is appropriate here to mention Dr. Esti Lavi, who through her questionings made me start to formulate my thoughts. Thanks to Dr. Yoram Kaufman, Nili Miller, Marianne Weinberg, Rivka Feit, Dr. Phyllis Schlemmer, Larisa Ronis, Lea Lipschitz and Danit Beer.

Dr. Carolyn Conger, Dr. Hal and Sidra Stone were the instigators of a new phase of development for me. Their work in Voice Dialogue and the Psychology of Selves opened a new experiential dimension to my inner and outer work. It also coincided with the formulation of my thoughts, enriching and validating them. Our years of friendship are valued.

Very special thanks go to Hanni Binder. She has proved to be a constant friend with unflinching support. She has been a rock in my professional life as a Jungian-oriented therapist. It was through her that I got to know Dr. Robert Hinshaw.

The ideas of the book were conceived over a dinner with Sylvia Perera in New York. It was her suggestion and persistency that prompted the writing until it reached its present form. I am grateful to her for her constructive comments, as well as for her warm friendship. It is a friendship that deepens and ripens with the years.

My appreciation goes to my friend and eldest daughter, Adi Wenderow-Ganani, who encouraged me through all the ups and downs of the writing, as well as to my youngest daughter Carmela for her patience, and to all my other friends who accompanied me.

Very special thanks go to Dr. Robert Hinshaw, who directed me to the final version of this book, and to Audrey Haas, who helped in the editing and typing of the manuscript, for bearing with me through the labors of this birth. Her amiable and long-standing friendship is cherished.

I thank Sergio Bustamante for permitting the use of his "Tingambato" for the cover.

Last but not least my gratitude goes to my dear husband Miki – without him this book would not have been materialized. His presence and support are invaluable.

Yael Haft-Pomrock

Preface

This book is a compilation of the results of more than thirty years of my work as a psychochirologist. Looking at the psyche chirologically, I found that new meanings emerge from old ideas and connections of archetypal images to patterns of behavior. I want to share with you my ideas and findings as they proved to be helpful throughout my work, to clinicians in the various fields of psychotherapy, to my pupils, clients, patients and to myself.

The purpose of my book is to open up different and deeper perspectives that may help us understand non-verbal phenomena via our hands. This is readily available to us once we learn the language. It is not a manual of "how to," but a pointer to another vehicle that may help all those who take upon themselves the service of helping others on their way.

My point of reference to the deeper meaning of the hand is based on the hypothesis that the hand portrays the workings of the archetypes within the personality. My aim is not to "prove" this hypothesis but to accept this premise, use it and expand it in order to understand the relationship of the working of the opposites in the personality within themselves and with each other as well as their possible complementariness.

Mythological themes and figures can be applied to the hand, as the hand is a micro-picture of the macro-psyche, just as a single cell holds within it the whole organism. This theory opens a new field of observation for the psychologist to become aware of. For, just as psychology helped me comprehend chirology in a far deeper and richer manner, so did chirology teach me about psyche.

As we all know, our psyche is intricate and elusive. While writing this book, I found that at times clear and simple language does not do justice to the full understanding of the workings of the archetypes. It loses something vital. I reverted then to the use of imaginal archetypal language to get to the "feel" of their intricacies. It will, perhaps help to sense their forces when joined for and also against each other.

Our hands are the only organ in our body that we can fully turn, utilize, inspect as an almost separate entity. To have our psyche "printed" in this vital organ as it is, is like an invitation. "Here I am what I am."

I. A Brief History

Of all the living creatures, only the human and the chimpanzee have hands. The hand of the chimpanzee is, however, undeveloped, especially the thumb. The process of human evolution from the primates is closely related to the evolution of our hands, a marvellous organ that has developed in unison with our brain as though externalizing its activity.

The common denominator between the skin and nervous system is the formation of these tissues in the ectoderm of the embryo.[1] Of all skin surfaces, those of the hands and face are the most sensitive and are subject to the greatest exchange between inner and outer stimuli. The hands and mouth occupy the largest areas in the medula of the brain.

From the earliest developmental stages of the infant, we can discern the hands in constant motion with the mouth, coordinating, opening and closing. There appears to be a close connection between ego development and the infant's increasingly finer differentiation in using the hand; in other words, our inner construction of reality and hand manipulation.[2] Together with the strengthening of the ego, the hand becomes more expressive and the inner palm shows its lines more clearly, although they are defined at birth. The hand portrays a measure of

1. Dr. Pierre Soliman, oral communication to author, 1968
2. N. Cameron, *Personality, Development and Psychotherapy,* (Boston: Houghton-Mifflin, 1963), pp. 48-50

development for both the individual and the species, in that the higher the differentiation of the ego, the more curved and complex the lines of the palm become.[1]

Handprints were made in the caves of Lascaux some twenty thousand years ago. They are found by crawling through a narrow opening to reach the far end of a cave, as though the passage may have meant a second birth into the consciousness of "I am, and my handprint is my signature."

During the reign of the Egyptian pharaoh, Amenophis IV from 1375 to 1358 B.C., Atum, the One God, was depicted as a sun disc with rays emanating in hands, implying a connection between this acting organ and God's action in the life-giving power of the sun's rays. The hieroglyph for the word "ka" meaning "vital force" is two raised hands.

The same motif is in Exodus 17:11, "And it came to pass, when Moses held up his hand that Israel prevailed; and when he let down his hand, Amalek prevailed." Raising the hand is the means by which we receive God's power and blessing. Michelangelo expressed this most beautifully in the Creation of Adam in the Sistine Chapel.[2] At the moment of creation, the hands of God and of Adam separate, the energy flowing from God to Adam through the fingers.

Chiromancy comes from two words: "Chiro" meaning hand, and "mancy" meaning divination. This is the origin of relating chiromancy to "fortune-telling." It deals mainly with prediction using the mantic arts. It was linked with astrology and esoteric knowledge, becoming the forerunner of chirology.

Chirology means the "logos" of the hand, i.e., the "language," the "knowledge" or "wisdom" of the hand. It

1. Dr. Hugo Debrunner, oral communication to author, 1964
2. I owe this comment to Rivka Feit who drew my attention to it.

deals with inner psychic processes, thus forming a thread linking the Kabalah, Gnosticism, alchemy and modern archetypal psychology. Chirology, in reflecting the psychic structure in the body, lays the responsibility for conscious growth on the active participation of the ego, as in the analytical process.

Recorded testimonies on historical chiromancy in the West are very scarce. The first written reference is to be found in the work of Aristotle, "De Historia Anaimalium," in which he says that all that is man is revealed in his hand. Anaxagoras also believed that the supremacy of man came to him through the use of his hand. One of the first basic manuscripts on chiromancy, which is kept in the British Museum, is called, "Summa Chiromantia" and its author is probably Johannes, who lived in the 14th century. The appearance of chiromancy in Europe is assigned to Avicenna, an Arab doctor and philosopher of that century. At that time, chiromancy was practised and studied by doctors and was, in fact, a branch of medicine. By the 15th and 16th centuries, Bartholemy Cocles, who was a physician, surgeon, mathematician and astrologer, advised all physicians and surgeons to study the hands of their patients.

Paracelsus, the Renaissance Swiss doctor and researcher, used to examine hands to diagnose illnesses, and he taught this method to his students. Coclenius continued Paracelsus' studies and taught them at the University of Wittemberg. In England, another pupil of Paracelsus, Robert Fludd, believed that psyche and soma are one and spread the diagnostics of his teacher to that island. In the 17th century, chiromancy was part of the medical curriculum in the universities of Leipzig, Dresden, Jena and Oxford.

In the Age of Reason, in the Cartesian division of Western academic learning into science and the humanities, it was discarded from scientific studies. Nonetheless, the mystery of the hand impressed the distinguished English physician, Sir Charles Bell, as he emphasized its connection with the autonomous nervous system and the related parts of the brain. The inner urge to know what lies hidden in the lines, that are so personal and unique, is reflected in the title of his book, published in 1833, "The Hand, Its Mechanism and Vital Endowments, an Evincing Design."

In the 19th century, three chirologists developed the theories that have formed the basis of the rebirth of modern chirology. Casimir Stanislas d'Arpentigy, wrote, "La Chirognomie," in 1839, compiling the six basic types of hands in use to this day. Desbarrolle wrote "Les Mystères de la Main," in 1859, showing the influence of the Kabalah and of Chaldean-Gnostic ideas on which his theory is based: the three worlds of the matter, the psyche and the spirit.[1]

Carl Gustav Carus, a physician and university professor who lived until 1869, and whose influence Jung acknowledges in his psychiatric training, wrote, "Ueber Grund und Bedeutung der Verschiedenen Formen der Hand," (Concerning the Foundation and Meaning of the Different Forms of the Hand) and "Die Symbolik der Menschlichen Gestalt" (The Symbolism of Human Forms) and "Psyche." He based his theory on the function of the hand and its application to various types of characteristics. His basic idea of the interrelatedness of soma and psyche, in which "each form in the organism is derived from infinite repetitions of the first fertilized ovum... (and) every cell has a life of its own,"[2] shows that an organism is a dynamic

1. F. Getting, *The Book of the Hand,* (London: Hamlyn, 1965), p. 176. The above data is taken from this work
2. C.G. Carus, *Psyche* (Part I, On the Development of the Soul), (Zurich & New York: Spring Publications, 1971), p. 18

field of relationships between cells that form, decay and form anew, subordinated in the process to a higher unity.

According to Carus, the development of the embryo through the various stages already bears within it the determinants of the individual's soma-psyche relations with the world. In his words, "the entirely unconscious functions responsible for the growth and form of the organism as an embryo are connected to consciousness in that they create organs which later receive, retain and modify images."[1]

He postulates that, "... the nervous system is purely of the soul."[2] And the organs most related to the nervous system are the organs of sense and movement, that is, the hands.

Carus elaborated his two-type theory of the function of the hands: the asthenic cerebral, which is predominantly tactile and includes feelings and sensitivity; and the athletic-motoric, which is prehensile and includes movement and grasping. So we have the tactile, which he further subdivides into the sensitive and the psychic hands; and the prehensile, which subdivides into the elementary and the motoric hands.[3]

An interesting parallel (cited by Getting) to these basic types and sub-types, is to be found in the Chinese theory of the hands. The elementary type is called the "hand of the Earth"; the motoric hand is called the "hand of wood"; the sensitive hand, the "hand of water"; and the psychic hand, the "hand of metal."[4]

I base my work on the theories of Julius Spier and Hugo Debrunner. Dr. Debrunner, a chirologist, psychiatrist and neurologist lived in Switzerland. He had his own

1. *Ibid.*, p. 6
2. *Ibid.*, p.35
3. F. Getting, *op. cit.*, p. 33
4. *Ibid.*, p. 35

theories based on physiology. He was concerned mostly with dermatogliphics, the fingerprints and patterns in the palm, as well as the main lines and their form. There is still a wealth of information to be discovered in these patterns, which are structural psychic characteristics that never change and have to be understood. I am also indebted to Charlotte Wolff,[1] who was the first to base her research in hospitals on the scientific measurements of the hands and correlate them to different physical and mental illnesses. Wolff elaborated on Carus' theories by subdividing the prehensile into four subtypes and the tactile into long and short hands; and all hands into wide and narrow hands. All three are closely founded on Carus.

1. Charlotte Wolff, *The Human Hand* (London: Methuen 1942) and *The Hand in Psychological Diagnosis* (New York: Philosophical Library, 1952)

II. Introduction to Archetypal Chirology

In the Zohar it is written:

> "... the hands of man are forms and higher mysteries that God put in man, and arranged them in the fingers outside and inside, and in the palm of the hand... and God, when He created man, arranged in him all the forms of the high mysteries of the lower world, and these mysteries are imprinted in man that was created in God's image. And, therefore, he was called 'palm-creation,' meaning 'the creation of God's palm.' "[1]

It is for us to try to become aware of these mysteries which hold essential psychological meaning for each one of us.

It was Julius Spier, working with Jung, who emphasized the psychological dynamics of the hand, rather than the functional dimension; he called his theory "Psychochirology." Jung, in his introduction to Julius Spier's book, "The Hands of Children: An Introduction to Psychochirology," writes that:

> "... the totality conception of modern biology... and research does not exclude the possibility that hands, whose shape and functioning are so intimately connected with the psyche, might provide revealing and therefore interpretable expressions of psychical peculiarity, that is, of the human character."[2]

1. M. Bakal, ed. (n.d.): The Book of the Wisdom of the Hand: Taken from the Zohar (Jerusalem)
2. J. Spier, *The Hands of Children: an Introduction to Psycho-Chirology*, (London: Routledge & Kegan Paul, 1944), Preface.

What is understood as the human character is in fact the realization of two distinct factors: the structure of the personality, which is a given that cannot be changed, just as much as the structure of our physiognomy cannot be changed, unless by external intervention such as operations of face and body or active therapies such as bioenergetics or rolfing. The second factor is the dynamic process of life experiences, introjections of important figures, defence mechanisms that we have adopted to avoid pain and the dynamic functioning of the archetypes working within. All these can at times make us hide or distort our basic structure.

Chirologically, the structure of the personality can be seen in the forms of the hands and fingers. Its dynamic aspects reveal themselves in the expression, position and relationships of the back of the hand and the fingers, as well as in the lines and mounts in the inner palm, as we shall see in the chapters to come.

I took in my work three of Spier's five basic forms, the conic, the square and the spatulate, and added a fourth one, which I use from Ursula von Mangold,[1] the oval. I omitted Spier's "philosophical" and "dysplastic" forms, as the former is, in fact, a combination of the conic, square and what I call oval forms and the latter is one or more of the basic forms in the palm and a combination of all the forms, in that each finger belongs to a different one. I came to this conclusion from my experience. None of the forms exist purely as such in reality; usually one finds combinations and variations of the basic forms.

In classical chirology only male archetypes were depicted in the fingers – with the exception of Venus and Luna in the inner palm. I was never content with this concept

1. Ursula von Mangold, *Zeichen des Schicksals im Bild der Hand, Anlagen und Möglichkeiten* (Olten/Freiburg im Breisgau: Walter-Verlag, 1961), pp. 57-61

of Venus and the Moon as the sole feminine archetypes. It occurred to me: Why not add the feminine counterparts to the masculine archetypes referred to in classical chirology. I took up mythology and was fascinated to find that I could immediately correlate it with chirological findings, which gave me immediate assurance that I was going the right way. Since 1970 I started working with the feminine counterparts, as well as the masculine in the hand and I found that they coincided to a remarkable extent with the personality traits.

The idea of seeing in the fingers and in the mounts of the inner palm, the archetypal images, i.e., the Gods and Goddesses, enables us to become aware of the inherent faculties, tendencies and possibilities within the archetypes as such. In the words of James Hillman[1] "there is always a God in what we are doing"... and "The Gods are the archetypal premises within all experience and all attitudes."

Marie-Louise von Franz says:[2] "The Gods are representations of certain natural constants of the unconscious psyche, of the ways in which the emotional and imaginative elements of the personality behave." Thus they can serve for inner growth and transformation and increase the experience and expressions of whatever there is in the various archetypal images within the person's capability at any given time.

The archetypes contain all the modes and levels of existence, from the gross, basic level or stage up to the highest and sublime ones. They manifest themselves in each individual in a personal way. By becoming aware of their manifestations, we can also become conscious of the

1. James Hillman, *Re-Visioning Psychology* (New York: Harper & Row, 1975), p. 227
2. Marie-Louise von Franz, *Number and Time* (London, Rider & Co., 1974), pp.31-32

possibilities of evolving within the archetypal realm from wherever we are at a certain time in our history to other, higher levels of the archetype. Each archetypal image has various characteristics, both in its positive and negative aspect. The opposites are always there. By recognizing the archetypal image behind the complex working within, we are one step away from it and we can transcend things as they are or appear to be from a more or less "static" state to a new phase of understanding and insight.

By perceiving the myths of archetypal images that appear in the fingers and mounts in the inner palm, we can then enlarge our knowledge of possible unconscious ways of behavior that dominate our lives. The myths are archetypal scenarios that rule us in more ways than we realize, as long as we are oblivious to their impact on our lives.

My most recent ideas pertain to the oppositions within archetypes and between archetypes, appearing in the fingers and mounts. I was intrigued with the question: Is there oneness beyond these opposites? A transcendent oneness that completes the opposition? By "complete" I mean wholeness that includes the opposites but goes beyond, usually with the aid of a third factor. What is found is that the opposites always come together, one cannot be without the other; the completion is not apparent. We can say, then, that completion may be the missing element in the opposites.

Our very conception prior to our birth into the oppositions of reality, is an outcome of the unification of opposites, man and woman in the act of love, ovum and sperm forming a foetus, foetus and womb in unison and opposition. So, our very essence is imbued with the archetype of oneness, the "echo" of the moment of union, and its "shadow" side as opposition. The one spliting into others, from the formation of cells to organs, nerves, characteristics, behavioral patterns, ego and inner parts, ego and world, ego and self. Our very act of being created into this world is a journey through oppositions where wholeness and oneness act as a striving force towards that utopian idea underlying ultimate oneness and completion beyond the opposites. This, in fact, is the most profound dynamic that operates in us on all levels of our being, outwardly and inwardly in all the facets of our life.

I had concentrated on the interplay between the left and right hands. Julius Spier out of his vast experience contends that in a right-handed person the right hand pertains to the parental images, what he calls the "ancestral" hand, and the left hand is the hand of the individual personality. In a left-handed person it will be the reverse, namely, the right hand will personify one's own individuality and the left hand the ancestral images working within. Spier's use of the word "ancestral" is based on the fact that our lives and patterns of character and behavior are linked to our ancestors and immediate family, that we either inherit, genetically, were influenced by, or introjected and interpreted. Having them portrayed in the predominant hand emphasizes and shows how their activity works within ourselves. Often we are unaware of how our inner parental figures determine our lives, and how easily we unconsciously take upon ourselves unresolved problems of our parents, thus not really living our own lives, but continuing theirs. Our own individual self is, so to speak, in our "passive" hand pointing to the "opus" of our life; to make "active" our own individual personality by differentiating and becoming conscious of what is one's own and what pertains to the parental images working within us.

As observed in the hospital while doing research on schizophrenia, this distinction came out in the case studies, that the parental figure (right hand) was confirmed even in outer reality (when the therapist met the parents). The pathology was sometimes even more accentuated in the right, parental, hand, but the carrier of the family pathology was the person whose hands I was analyzing. This finding correlates with Arieti's[1] and Laing's[2] contention that a sick person is often the carrier of the illness of another family member, mother or father, who are "schizophrenogenic," or, that he represents a sick family.

Often we consciously try to be different and to live differently than one or another of the parental figures, not realizing that by so doing we continue to do to ourselves what the parent, whom we tried so hard to "exclude" from our lives, did to us. We unconsciously may marry someone who personifies this parental figure, or meet these figures in our life again and again. Usually the two hands are different, one from the other, both in the form of the palm and the fingers, their expression and the way the fingers relate to each other, as well as the lines on the inner palm. This implies the dynamic aspect of conflict arising out of these oppositions and points to their possible complementariness. Where conflict arises lies the possibility for change and transformation but when the differences between the hands are too great the inner conflicts can be devastating.

The more similar the hands are, the less the conflict between the parents and between them and the person. This will convey the need to follow the road well-travelled of the parents and continue in the same pattern. It also points to repetitions of characteristics and behavior and for generational repetitions of problems. Similarity can also be difficult at the stages of maturation, i.e., in childhood and adolescence.

1. Silvano Arieti, *Interpretation of Schizophrenia,* 2nd ed., (New York: Basic Books, 1974)
2. Ronald Laing, *The Self & Others: Further Studies in Sanity and Madness* (London: Tavistock Publications, 1961)

The ability to assess parental images, influences and relationships in our own hands, provides a useful tool for the understanding of parent and also child bonding that continues to operate into our own adult lives. We can never run away from our parental images – they are within us. We can, however, learn to utilize differently and maybe transform their archetypal characteristics and patterns of behavior within us.

It may be the first time that the person meets the parents as people with their own problems, pathologies and suffering. Just as frequently, the lived or unlived potentialities of the parental images can add to the understanding of a drive within the person. Having them in our own hand potentiates their capability to become available to us. It is derived from the parental, yet disowned within us.

As I went deeper into the mythical figures, I realized that I might be led by them into a more differentiated understanding of the type of psychology that rules a person at a certain time, and its significance to the therapeutic process. I call them Patterns of the Internal Familial layout as portrayed by the fingers.

The first finger, portraying Zeus/Hera, relates to the couple. They symbolize the archetype of the couple[1]: husband and wife. Our stand in the world is connected to this archetype which is the structured foundation of society. The basic need of each one of us to be married, to have a wife or husband, in order for us to feel secure in our dealings with the world and in the "inner world" within us. Taken on an internal level, it points to the inherent necessity to be "married" to our inner wife/husband, i.e., to our inner contrasexual part.

1. Karl Kérenyi, *Zeus and Hera: Archetypal Images of Father, Husband and Wife* (Princeton University Press, Bollingen Series LXV, 5, 1975), pp. 53 ff.

The second finger, Saturn/Athena, relates to the adult, wise old man and to the eternal youth (not child), Senex and Puer – be it feminine or masculine. Our thinking, therefore, belongs in fact to the adult or 'grown-up'-part of us (in the sense that to be "grown-up" is to act reasonably), because it holds within it the potential for an independent, responsible thinking function.

The third finger, Apollo/Artemis, brings out the free man and woman in each of us. Our feeling values and clarity of sight and the ability to analyze belong to our need for freedom and independence. We can be impersonal in our clear seeing-through, free to dance the dance of life, or very personal in our feeling judgments. We can imprison ourselves as dutiful, pleasing or rebellious and defiant daughters or sons – in captivity or in bondage – portraying the psychology of the son/daughter, personified by Persephone, as shadow figure to Artemis.

The child in all of us is connected to the fourth finger, Hermes/Mercury. He can be childish, shy, playful, ingenious or compliant, submissive, crushed, fearful, rejected and unwanted. He is always vulnerable and very often in pain. Our whole life depends on this energy. The child is the carrier of the Self as he appears symbolically. He holds the essence of our being and is therefore the activating force in our personality. We cannot reach our "core" without first integrating, by accepting, our child in all its vulnerability. The child never grows up – he does not need to grow. He always represents the possibility of renewal or of finding new ways.

Our thumb represents the ego as the carrier of consciousness: the ability to differentiate, to will, to choose and to execute. He is the one who can make use of the different aspects of our inner "family," without negating the experience of these inner figures, and the one who can accept, let be and become aware of their manifestations. He can hold the opposite inherent within the images themselves, as well as the oppositions between the fingers and the archetypal images located in the palm of our hands. The more aware the ego becomes, the more these parts of energy patterns can transform within themselves.

I am amazed at the inner law of opposites as it is laid out in our hands. The order of the archetypal images as they are located in the fingers and in the palm opposite each other portrays how they are connected in their manifestations, both positively and negatively. They are also influenced by their neighbors but the connection is within the location, so to speak: this cannot be separated, it can only be faced and acknowledged, like a given decree. These ideas have come to fruition in a theory of an inner law imprinted in the hand. They opened to me new venues of understanding of inner psychic patterns that I could incorporate in my work as a therapist.

Opposites intensify each other, either by joining forces in complementation or by combatting each other. They operate on all levels or only on some levels. The key to the opposition does not lie in the transmutation of these instinctual powerful energies, to do this would cause further splitting of the opposites. To transmute the energies even to a higher plane cannot be done, because by averting them one loses the experience which can be very important, although difficult, for one's development. Suppressing an archetypal energy makes it become lethal, demonic and evil. Suppressing the principle of natural growth, which is inherent in the life force, might cause it to go into a "wild" growth, like cancer, or an epidemic. Whatever we have in our hands, we have for a purpose, for example fear as opposed to love. The idea is not to eliminate anything.

Fear is needed for our survival, so too is anger. Anger is a necessary emotion when wrong has been done: anger as protest, as stamina for change. Jealousy can serve as a signpost for the things we want and are not allowed, either by ourselves or others, or the things we deny or disown. All of these, and others, are the means whereby we may become aware of the need for transformation. As James Hillman says:

> The archetypes... like the Gods, rule all at once and together the same realm of being, this our world. But they provide distinction within this world, different ways of regarding things, different patterns for psychizing instinct, different modes of consciousness.[1]

1. James Hillman, "The Great Mother, her Son, her Hero and the Puer" in *Fathers and Mothers*, ed. by Patricia Berry (Dallas: Spring Publications, 2nd ed., 1990), p. 185

III. The Forms of the Hand

My premise is that within each form of one's hands, there is hidden the missing element, the clue for that person to become whole. The form of our hands is genetically ordained; it cannot be changed. What can be changed is within the process of the psychic structure, signified by the contents of each form.

The mirroring of the psyche in our hands, as we shall see, shows us that we come into this world for a reason. Yet very early in life, already in utero, during and after birth, we start reacting to environmental influences via our parents and life circumstances. They may be in opposition to the inherent reason for our life, i.e., becoming what we were born to be. We cannot be otherwise than what we are, and it is a fundamental law that we must live either the positive or negative aspect of our traits. If we live them outwardly as the negative side, then the shadow contains the positive aspect of this trait.

To sort out the meanings of the words I shall be using as a Jungian-oriented therapist, I perceive the difference between "awareness" and "consciousness" as the difference between knowing something and actually experiencing the significance of this knowing. Psychotherapy is to become aware of the whole spectrum of our structure. It is an opportunity for both awareness and consciousness of the process of becoming whole. In the process of living, it is the opportunity to choose the enhancing characteristics, still unknown to us, that pertain to and exist within the form of the hands.

The four main types of hand-forms found in my thirty years of working with hands, show the basic overall characteristics of the personality.

The form is like a topography showing the ruling aspects operating within. Each form has within itself the key to the completion of the opposites operating within it. For example, each form has inherent active and passive components. The active component is designated "masculine" and the passive as "feminine," according to the classic stereotypic divisions. The radial part of the hand, thumb, first (index) finger and part of the second finger, is the *active* part of the hand; it is flexible and usable and is more connected to the sympathetic nervous system and is therefore considered to be the conscious part of the hand. The ulnar side, the other part of the second finger and the third and fourth fingers, is considered to be the *passive,* unconscious side.

So, within the whole, we have the parts; the feminine-passive and masculine-active sides. Within this opposition we have the middle finger that holds both parts; this finger "holds the two together" in actuality. The second (middle) finger is usually higher than the other fingers, thus showing the elevated possibility of holding the opposites and balancing them. It points, in this respect, to the key to the complement, the higher point of view and the balancing scale between the opposites. When speaking of the forms of the hand the thumb was not included. Its role lies in being outside the form.

a) The Conic Form

The conic form suggests a triangle; it is wider at the base, uniting at a higher point. The triangle has a dynamic aspect, pointing forward like an arrow, a "masculine" element. Owners of such a hand-form are usually people who tend to extremes and change like a pendulum that swings from one side to the other; they are very impressionable and labile. They are reactive in their behavior, are very susceptible and sensitive, easily influenced and receptive – the classic designations of "feminine." So we have within the form and its owner both masculine and feminine components: masculine in the form itself and feminine in its attributes. Among owners of such a hand, we find artists, dancers, actors and musicians.

More than in any other form, the middle finger of the conic is long and serves as the apex of the triangle. In addition to the middle finger's function as stabilizer in general, the middle finger in this form serves as the key to wholeness, in that it is the pendulum causing the extremes in the lability of the owner's personality. Therefore, in its function as the spine of the hand, the middle finger as the high point, especially in the conic form, can serve as a focus of the owner's varied impressions, which is usually lacking.

The third element synthesizing the opposition, lies in the *tonus* of the hand. The tonus gives our personality support, resilience, weakness or rigidity. The tonus serves as the vehicle for our psychic attitude towards ourselves and others. Through it we can learn about modes of openness or closure, such as fluidity (when someone shakes your hand and it seems to be melting) or rigidity, indicating the inter- and intra-defence mechanisms.

The conic form as a masculine symbol can add a masculine basis to the feminine personality traits, merging the yang and yin energies. The opposition of active and receptive can become complementary using the psychic structure indicated by the middle finger: cultivating the thinking ability that provides a higher view over things; seeking a structural "middle column" for the sways in lability and a "spine" to keep the individual grounded, yet upright. In the conic hand this functioning of the middle finger is of paramount importance in the psychic structure to achieve wholeness, although it functions in this mode in every hand-form.

b) The Square Form

This form is rectangular, denoting fixed boundaries. The four sides represent a ground, a matrix, which is a feminine symbol. This hand-form belongs to persons who are orderly, bound to facts and figures, to regulations, conventions and laws. The term "a square person" is relevant. Such persons need to verify things; they are not easily impressed or influenced. They are active, yet steady. These characteristics personify what are designated as "masculine" components. Again we have "femininity" in the form and "masculinity" in the attributes.

The key to wholeness for persons with this form of hand lies in the thumb. The ability to will, decide and execute is signified by the thumb, which is therefore a somatic indicator of ego capability. The ground (the palm of the hand), as it is fixed and bound, needs the active ego to become whole; otherwise it is caught in inertia and stagnation. The feminine needs the masculine for action.

The masculine attributes of persons who have a square hand lack openness and a capacity to flow with things. Often they need some feminine elements in their personality as a "rounding of the square." The curve is feminine and fluid, denoting the receptivity that the square-handed person sometimes lacks.

A flexible, even slightly soft hand tonus will give this hand a softening of character, the needed feminine element. The necessary curve can sometimes be found in the ulnar side of the palm, "moisturizing" so to speak, this strict, fixed and dry form.

c) The Oval Form

This form is egg-shaped and, like an egg, it points to the possibilities of incubation. From an egg something always emerges. The curved shape gives a sense of fullness to the form. The shell of the egg is hard, but the inside is soft and liquid. The egg as a symbol combines within itself the opposites of hardness and softness, as well as exterior and interior. People whose hands are this shape always have a need to do something new. They go from one enterprise to the next; they need to be "on the go" in their searches and appetites. Once a target has been reached, they look for a new one. They lose interest in things or people, once they seem to know them. This can also lead to being fascinated with the external facets of whatever they are involved with, neglecting the internal content. They may become like the shell of the egg, hard and superficial; they are bound to the persona, split off and unrelating to others.

The opposite may also be there; they may be too soft and unformed, stuck in the foetal state, the egg that never hatched. They tend to live in their fantasies of what they would have wished to do or to have been capable of doing, but never did. They become bound to mood swings, seem somehow always dissatisfied and lacking something. They often feel a sense of emptiness and meaninglessness. Their need for new ventures will comprise frequent changes of work or colleagues. They start things and leave them midway. They tend to feel that "that's not it," yet be unable to say what "it" is. Whereas everyone feels this way from time to time, in this type of person it is psychological block to becoming oneself, like the egg that did not mature.

The missing element, the key for completion in this case, is the incubation time: to be able to hold on, to look inward, to stay put in a situation and be interested in the search within for new developments, cultivating new forms or interests within the old, the already known, whether in work or in relationships.

The egg is also a container. In the ability to contain and to be contained lies the possibility for completion; the third element is found in the image of the form itself, the egg as a womb for things to gestate and ripen.

d) The Spatulate Form

This hand-form is like a shovel that can lift matter upwards from underneath. It has the shape of a spatula, narrow at the bottom and wider at the brim, as if it can hold things only to spread them out. Like any vessel, it is feminine in connotation.

Owners of hands of this shape are usually creative people in whatever they do. Creativity is a need, no matter what the endeavour. They also need acclaim for their deeds; it is essential to them. They can be considered "extrovert" in their focus on the outer world and on other people for expansion. They are "doers." In pushing themselves and others, they convey masculine or "yang" energy.

The key to completion lies in the feminine form of a holder, a container, of being instead of doing. This capability is shown in the softness of tonus and the curved outline in the ulnar side of the hand, as well as its curved inner lines.

There is also a reversed spatulate form. It is very wide at the base and less so at the top. Like a shovel, it tends to lift a lot of matter, but it will be unable to hold it, as it narrows at the top. This is characteristic of the hand of people interested in archaeology, anthropology, genetics, psychology and research pertaining to the origins of mankind. They connect us to the root of things. They may become engrossed in the search for beginnings and lose the overall view, unable to see the forest for the trees. They become trapped in the depths of whatever field they are in.

Whereas in the first spatulate form the key for completion lay in the feminine form as a container, the reversed spatula finds its completion in a third factor, the vivid expression of the hand, its resiliency, its consistency and a well-developed thumb to give it the "masculine" components of decision and execution, the ego force. Handforms can either complement or oppose each other. In the spatula and the inverted spatula, one is the complement to the other, one goes forward and the other goes back to beginnings.

In summary and conclusion, we have looked into the symbolic opposition and completion of the basic forms of the hands. However, these basic forms are not often encountered as such in actual life. Usually, we find mixed forms, such as conic-square, oval-square, oval-conic. They may complement each other, adding to the "missing" element something of what was needed: the conic, masculine form is complemented by the feminine, square form, pointing to an inherent possibility for integration. The impressionable, labile characteristics are counteracted and become milder with the addition of the squarish characteristics of order and boundaries.

It remains to be seen in the dynamics of the personality, as shown in the inner hand's lines and mounts, whether the inborn possibility for integration of both meanings of the basic forms is enhanced and complementary or diminished and conflictual.

IV. The Palms and Fingers

The palms and fingers adhere to the four basic forms: however we may have an oval form of palm and conic fingers, or even a square-oval palm (the oval side is usually the ulnar) with diverse forms of fingers – this combination is called "dysplastic."

Chirologically, the palm is the ground of our being, the primordial source, the "ur-grund." Mythically, we can call it our "Gaia," our Earth Mother. The palm is decisive in assessing the inherent liveliness, strength or weakness of the basic structure of the personality.

There is a story for the role of the fingers: The Earth goddess, Rhea, Meteri Oreia, "Mountain Mother," fled to Mount Ida to give birth to Zeus. Chronos (Saturn, or "Father Time") always swallowed her children. When the contractions became strong, she pressed her fingers into the earth, out of which sprang the Daktyloi, spirits and gods in the number of her fingers, who would always be at her service.[1] We may say the Daktyloi are the fingers of our hands serving the palm, our ground. This myth points to the esoteric understanding, even in ancient times, of the psyche-soma relationship.

Spier emphasized the relation between the fingers and the palm as this signifies the harmony or disharmony between the world of finitude, or matter, practicality and adjustability, and the world of the spirit, of ideas, intellect and imagination.

1. Karl Kérenyi, *The Gods of the Greeks* (London: Thames and Hudson, 1951), pp. 83-85

The palm is a fixed, finite form, bound on all sides – this is the world of actuality. The fingers are rooted and grow from it into space, open to receive and bring forth the fruit of new integration. The palm serves as a fundamental source of nourishment and sustainment.

The mythological images of the gods and goddesses that are designated to each finger, serve us as archetypal patterns and modes of behavior; they are also energy patterns. The upper mounts of the inner palm, being related to the fingers to which they are adjacent, correspond to their archetypes. The lower mounts, in the mid-palm and adjacent to the wrist, have archetypal meanings that differ from those of the fingers. These, as we shall see, pertain to the foundations of our being.

Debrunner divided the ulnar zone into two parts; the lower is subdivided into three layers. The one closest to the wrist pertains to the collective unconscious; the middle, to the personal unconscious; and the upper, to the outside or environmental unconscious influence. The higher part of the ulnar side pertains to relationships with others. (See diagrams, pp. 98-99)

The fingers are divided in their inner facet into three phalanges, except for the thumb which has only two. These three divisions denote the levels of existence in the world, as in Aristotle's cosmology. The lower part of the finger, the phalange next to the palm, represents the earthly aspect of basic needs, materialism and concreteness; the middle phalange represents practicality, common sense and rationality and the upper phalange, spirituality, abstract formulation and ideals. In the thumb, the upper phalange pertains to our will-power and power of execution and the lower to the thinking involved in discrimination and choosing.

The thumb determines the potential to discriminate, evaluate and suffer frustration. It is the "chirological seat of the I," the ego that wants, thinks, differentiates and executes. In the research into characteristics of schizophrenia as manifest in the hand, the thumb played a major role by its expression and quality. It is the dynamic agent involved in the activity of the psyche, its capabilities to create, to hold, to do and to become. It is the ego in the service of the Self. Its expression may change, whereas the potentiality sets its limits.

When I did the research on schizophrenia, I came to realize that the assessment of the outer palm is crucial and the only way to assess the strength or weakness of the palm is by its expression.

a) The Quality of Expression

Expression is vital in all forms of communication. It is the qualitative characteristic of energy.[1] As our hands communicate unconsciously who we are and what we are, their expression is part and parcel of the communication. Although it cannot be defined or measured, there is usually consensus as to designating modes of expression, such as "rigid," weak," "strong," "lively," "empty-looking" and "dead." There is even a concept I call "sealed," referring to strength, as though it were felt within the palm but it does not come out. Another quality, "active-passivity," conveys active energy not manifesting, as opposed to "passive-aggressive." The seed is inside, but something does not allow it to flourish. The lines of the inner palm may show there to be passive-aggressive traits but it may be that the fluidity that is within the deep earth does not nourish the fingers. To familiarize the reader with this terminology, we present the following photographs, progressing from lack of expression through various degrees of liveliness.

1. John Pierrakos, *Core Energetics* (New York: Life Rhythm Publications, 1987)

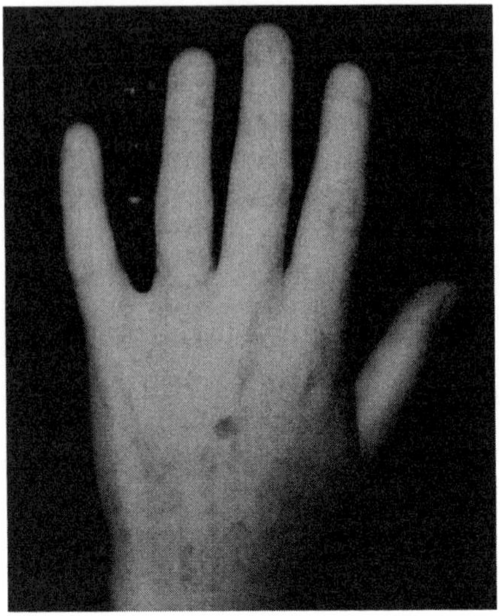

Picture 1. Lack of expression. Empty looking, both in the palm and fingers, except the 4th finger.

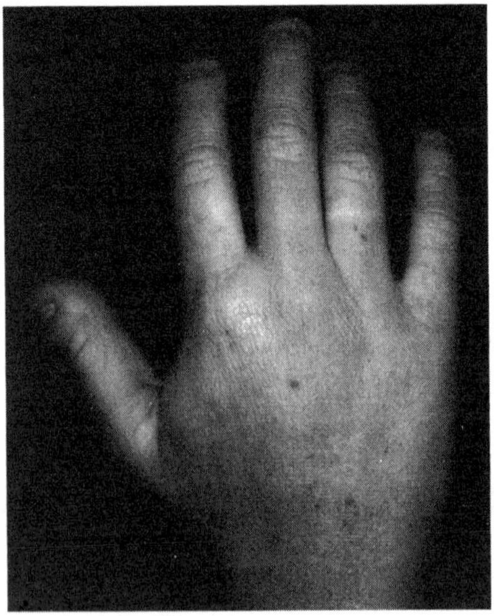

Picture 2. Lack of vitality, empty expression, undeveloped personality, crude.

right *left*

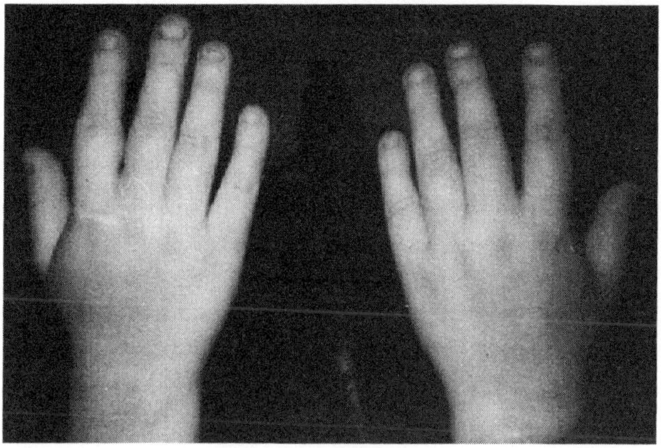

Picture 3. Weak expression, passive and undeveloped.

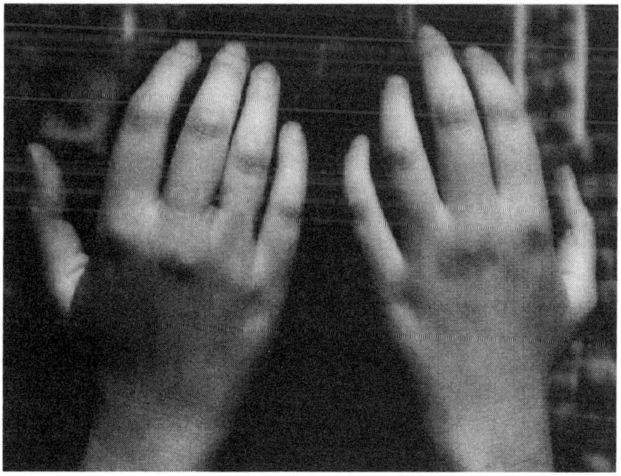

Picture 4. Very weak, passive, empty, lack of vitality.

right *left*

Picture 5. Weak expression, lack of vitality especially in the palm and thumb, empty.

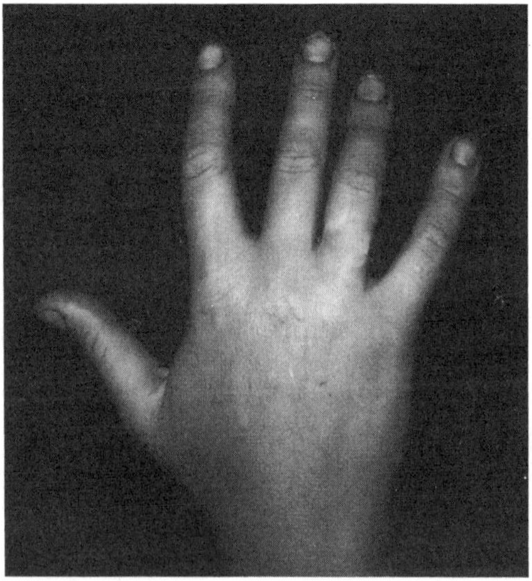

Picture 6. Empty palm, sealed strength. Expressive fingers.

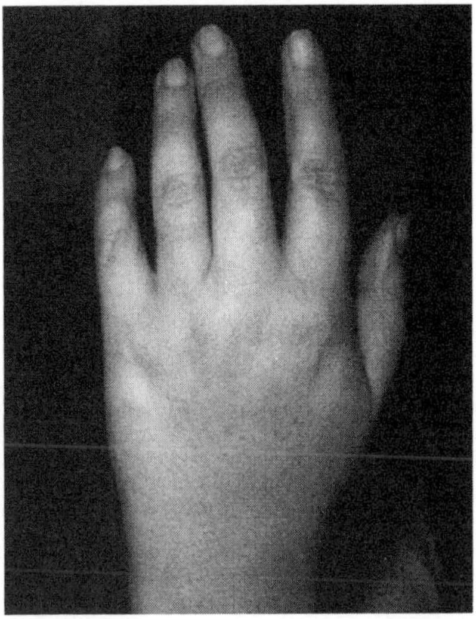

Picture 7. Weak, yet some liveliness, passive.

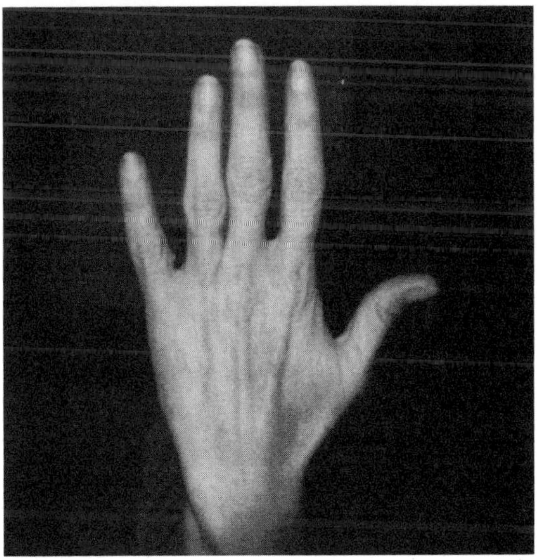

Picture 8. Lively expressive palm and fingers.

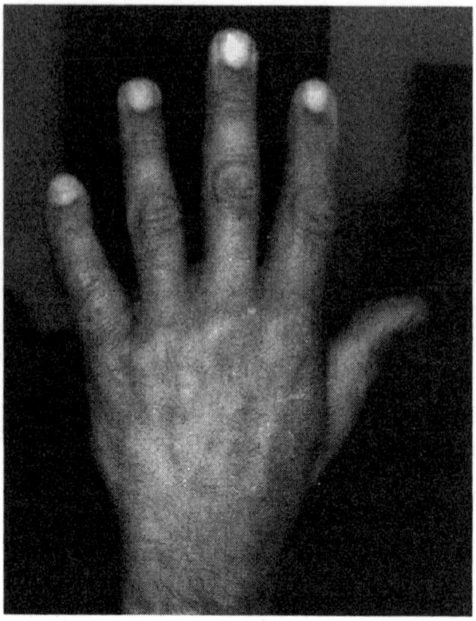

Picture 9. Stored liveliness in palm, active, expressive and strong fingers.

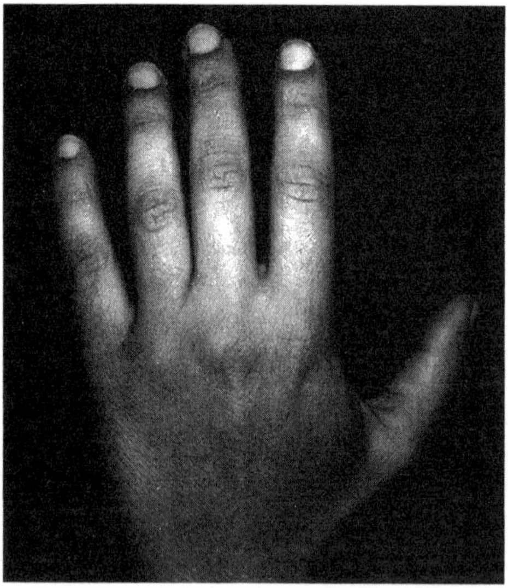

Picture 10. Rigidity and active passivity.

right *left*

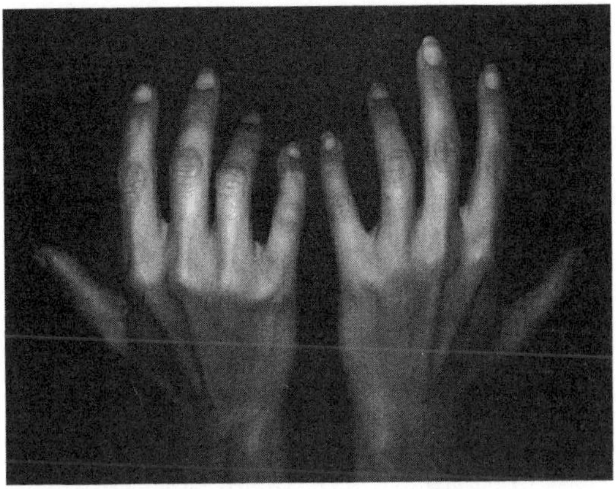

Picture 11. Lively and expressive palm and fingers.

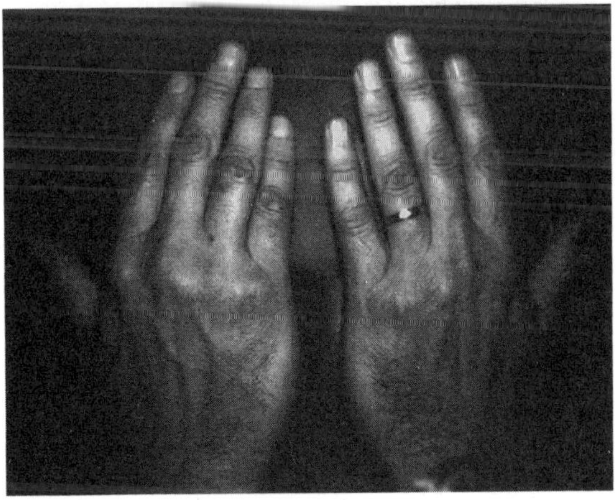

Picture 12. Lively, expressive and developed personality.

Inherent versus Current Expression

The more attuned we are to expressions, the more we can differentiate between the expressions of the fundamental inherent forces in the ground of our being, the force in the "Gaia" palm and also in the fingers. Yet there is another expression of the hand, as seen by the way one holds one's hands, lifted up from the elbows. This portrays the expression of the current psychic state.

b) Case Study in Inherent versus Current Expression

I first discovered the differentiation between the inherent expression of the outside of the hand and the current psychic state when a man of about thirty years of age came for a hand consultation. The different expression of his hands between the taking of the hand-prints and his holding them up on his elbows changed markedly without his being aware of it.

The procedure of the hand examination is first to take a print of the inner palm. This is done by smearing a special black ink on the palm and fingers with a roller, and then pressing the hands onto a sheet of paper. When the hands are on the sheet, just before the pressing, one can see the hands in their inherent expression, i.e., the expression of the structure. Then the person is asked to lift his or her hands, leaning the elbows on the table, the back of the hand facing the chirologist; this portrays the current psychic state.

It was so unusual to see such a difference – as if they were of two different people – that, at that time, I thought, "I must show it to him," so I photographed the two expressions.

The man reacted with astonishment when they were shown to him. Concerning the photograph in which he held his hand freely, he said: "This is how I am now, depressed, passive, weak." To the photograph in which he held his hand straight he said, "This is how I used to be, sure of myself, curious and optimistic." It was a momentous experience for him. It brought him to consider and undertake analysis in all seriousness.

Ever since that time, in the early seventies, I have been taking pictures of the difference between the current psychic state and the inherent forces within, for clients to whom this is relevant.

On the following pages we shall present examples of the expression of the present psychic state compared to the expressions of the inherent structure.

Expression changes as the psyche changes and is a measure of the therapeutic process of transformation. A weak expression of the palm shows direction for treatment in the strengthening of the basis of the personality. However, an "empty" expression of the palm can at times portray an irreversible pathological conditioning of the personality.[1] We may find expressive fingers with an expressionless palm that is either weak or rigid; this may indicate a lively archetypal image of potency but a barren or weak ground, a situation which may culminate in a psychosis. Or we may have the reverse – inexpressive fingers with an expressive, lively, motoric palm, meaning that the potentialities are not alive, although the ground is ready to "conceive."

1. Yael Haft-Pomrock & Yigal Ginath, M.D., Differences between Schizophrenics and Normal Controls using Chirological (hand) Testing. *Israel Journal of Psychiatry & Related Sciences,* Vol. 19, No. 1, 1982, pp. 5-22

right *left*

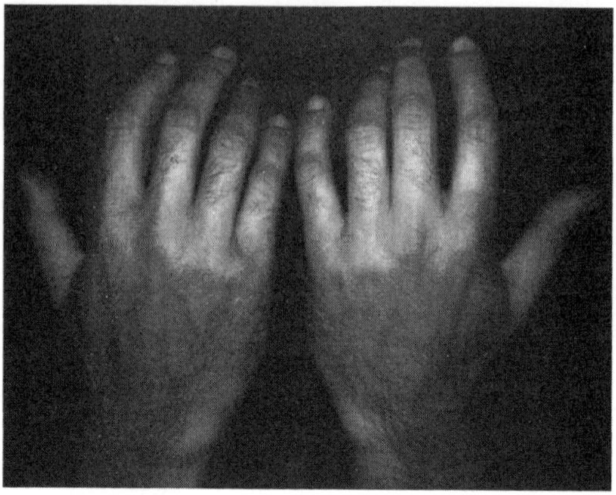

13. Expression of a present psychic state: weak, limp, depressed, especially the left hand. The thumb looks strong but passive. The fingers seem limp, especially the 3rd finger which looks "crushed" and under the middle finger.

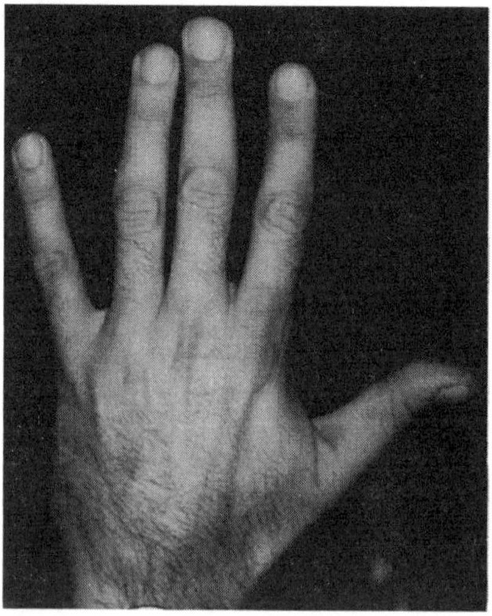

Picture 14. Expression of the structure of the left hand of the same person: lively palm and fingers. A strong and lively thumb.

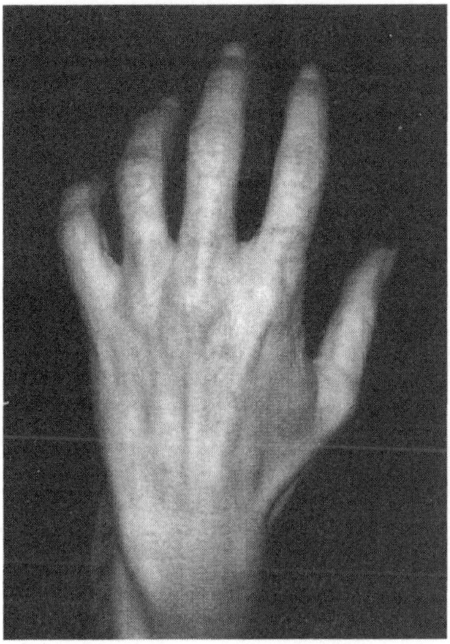

Picture 15. Present psychic state.

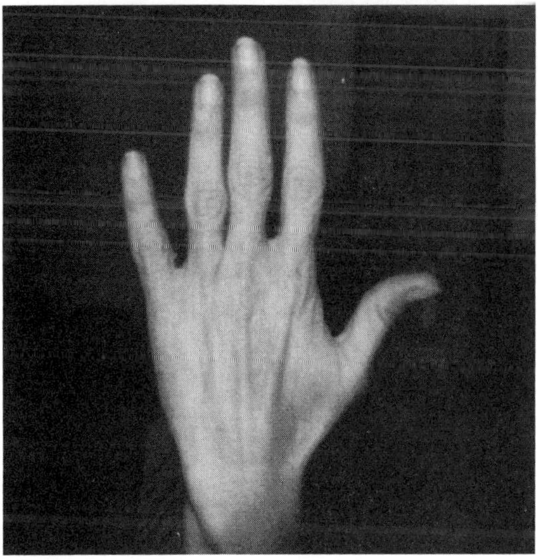

Picture 16. Inherent structure.

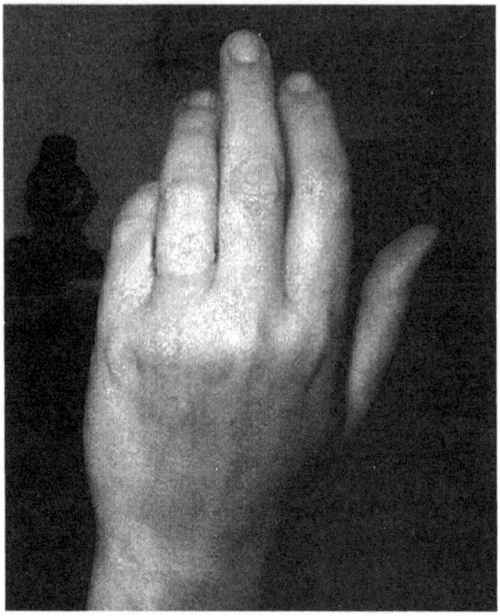

Picture 17. Present

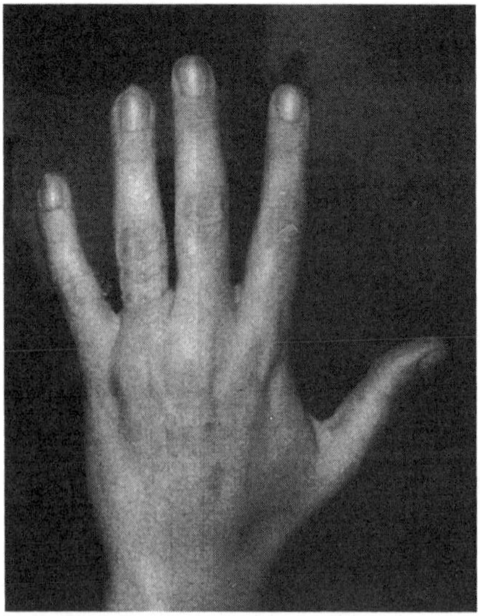

Picture 18. Inherent

c) Expression in the Archetypes and Forms

We will now refine the differentiation of expression to include that of the archetypes in the fingers and their four basic forms. Each finger in itself expresses an archetypal image with its specific functions and modes of behavior. The particular way a finger is positioned or is related to an adjacent finger, portrays the present mode of behavior or psychic state of an archetypal image. Expressions change: they represent psychic states, just as our body language can show psychic states.

On the *outside* of the hand, we assess the expression of the basis of the personality in the palm, and of the modes of behavior in the fingers, and the interplay of all together.

The *inherent* expression of the fingers is portrayed by the archetypes themselves. When the first finger is long and rectangular (the square form), it portrays the ability to rule, organize and be authoritarian; the Zeus archetype. Whereas, in the *current* expression: if a finger tends inward, even beneath the adjacent finger, and its expression is weak, the abilities of the archetype to which it pertains are curbed and under the influence of the adjacent archetypal forces. That means, if the first finger is bent and expresses weakness, there are feelings of inferiority, and when it is under the influence of the second finger the inferiority is under the harsh rule of the Saturn archetype. This shows the severity of the thought pattern attached to it. The outer aspects of the palm and fingers are regarded as the "archetypal layout," or inherent structure of the personality, whereas in the inside of the palm, the mounts and lines are the manifestations of its dynamic activity.

d) Archetypal Overview of the Meaning of the Fingers

In order to familiarize ourselves with the overall facets of the archetypal images as portrayed in the fingers, we shall specify them in the following pages. (Also see 'General Map of the Characteristics' on p. 98)

I found that the more experience one has in examining hands, the more it helps verify which of the gods and goddesses and which of their attributes are at work in a certain finger. We have them all to a varying degree. Consideration of other components of the hand, such as type of form and fingers, their expression, the lines in the inner palm, and in the mounts, will help to determine it. We can also study each finger from the vantage point of the archetypal images pertaining to the finger and see how each of them operates together or separately from the other, as will be shown in the sample consultations. Allowing as varied a spectrum as is relevant will add to a fuller and deeper assessment of the personality and the possibilities inherent within the archetype for transformation.

Index Finger – Zeus / Hera-Hestia

This is the finger belonging to the world, in Spier's words it is, "the finger of the world." It is connected to the "outside." It shows our way of dealing with outer reality, our orientation, adaptability, our power of observation, sense of perception, the use of our senses, our sense of organization, of domination, and ambition. It may have similarities with the function of sensation. It shows the way we handle and stand in the world – our world, whether inwardly or outwardly, whether in assurance or inferiority, whether forthcoming or holding back.

This first finger, which is the pointing finger, is the domain of Zeus, or Jupiter, and Hera is his feminine counterpart, also representing the couple. Both of them are collectively oriented and portray the need to rule. Zeus as emperor, king of the gods, symbolizes domination, self-assertion, administration, status-mindedness and expansion through conquest. The images of Zeus/Jupiter's attributes may well tell us in a more lively, pictorial way his functions, for example: "Thunderbolt" immediately brings to mind the image of the punishing finger, the accusing or threatening finger, which is the index finger. The crown and the throne can be looked upon as symbols of power and dominance, which can be seen in a long, expressive, strong index finger. The eagle, king of the birds, the spirit of the sun, is a spiritual principle – Zeus as prime mover. He symbolizes the patriarch in both positive and negative aspects. In Homeric times, Zeus symbolized the recurrent union of heaven and earth, yet somehow he was always secondary to the feminine power. His victories and power of domination are connected with the feminine by marriages and copulations, and in relations with both goddesses and mortal women.

We can say that our stand in the world, our feelings of superiority or inferiority, inner confidence or lack of it, and our ambitions and authoritative capabilities infect all spheres of our personality. They are deeply connected with and dependent upon our relationship to the basic feminine realms, to the goddess imago with her life-giving "milk," care and being – as well as her poisonous, devouring potions.

Before going on to the role of Hera in the first finger, however, I would like to say something about the whorl when found in the dermatoglyphics of a finger. This is a contribution from Debrunner's work which I have found extremely useful.[1] When there is a whorl  in the finger-

1. For further reading on Debrunner's work, see Hutchinson, Beryl B.: *Your Life in your Hands* (London: Neville Spearman, 1967), pp. 89-117

print, especially if it is to be found in every finger, that person is not determined by the collective but is a very individualistic person. To illustrate: if the whorl is in the first finger it indicates that in any work the person does, it is very important that he or she be in a position of a Zeus, i.e., be in command and responsibility, able to order their own way. In children, difficulties in learning may stem from the problems that they encounter in accepting the authority of a teacher; and in relationships, when this whorl is found in both partners in the first finger, power issues of dominancy can be one of the major problems between them. This is an opportunity for them to learn to respect each other's need for dominancy.

Hera the Queen, the patroness, the matron is the matriarchal authority in charge of and commanding schools, hospitals, institutions and family. Her main role is in propagating marriage and the family as a social institution. She is the protector of the wife, and goddess of childbirth but not of motherhood as such. According to the myth,[1] there are three facets to Hera. The first is Hera as a virgin, before marriage; here, she is called *"Parthenos,"* meaning young woman. Chirologically, the first finger's expression of eagerness or hesitancy, especially when the upper phalange is turned outward showing anticipation and curiosity, will tend to point to this phase.

In the *left hand,* Hera is in her Parthenos stage, the young woman with capabilities to rule – first finger hesitant, unsure (Picture 19).

In the *right hand* of the same Picture Jupiter/Zeus and Hera can also be seen, a presence of authority and sureness, representing the couple.

1. Karl Kérenyi, *Zeus and Hera* (Princeton, 1975), pp. 129 ff

right *left*

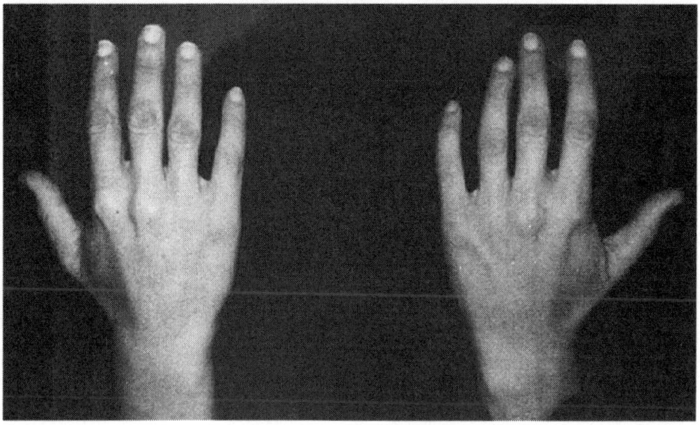

Picture 19

The second facet is Hera as *Tellia,* the married woman, but not necessarily the loving or loved one. She is possessive yet knows her own worth and her role as organizer and leader of the family or a group of people. This will be portrayed chirologically in a finger which is presented standing erect and expressing authority (Picture 20, left hand).

The third facet of Hera is called *Chera,* meaning widow or divorced woman. This portrays the woman who has experienced loss, widowhood, and is alone. It also portrays the rejected, neglected or lonely woman. As being divorced or widowed is still unfortunately considered a kind of social status, it is easy to identify with this archetypal state of being, which may obliterate the other aspects of Hera and Zeus (Picture 20, in the right hand). An example of Hera Chera can be seen in Picture 21. It portrays a state of mourning in both man and woman. Here, there is an expression of heaviness, sadness; sometimes standing slightly inward and away from the other fingers or bent in.

right *left*

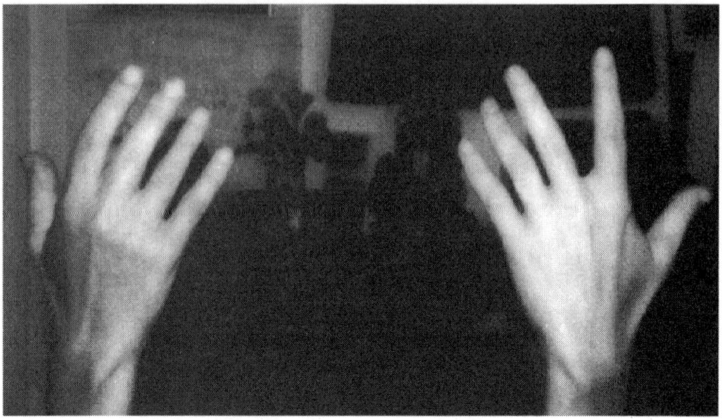

Picture 20. Tellia: First finger standing erect expressing authority.

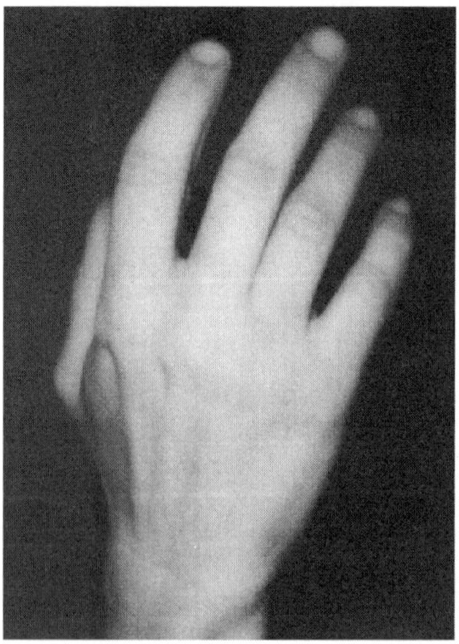

Picture 21. Chera: here there is an expression of heaviness, sadness, first finger standing slightly inward and away from the other fingers or bent in.

In their positive aspects both Zeus and Hera know their value and possess self-esteem and collective validation. In their negative aspects they personify tyranny and inconsideration. Hera is known for her vengeance, jealousy and vindictiveness. When the finger is very long, up to almost the second finger, it will convey this domination by tyranny, even up to hybris. (Picture 22, right hand.)

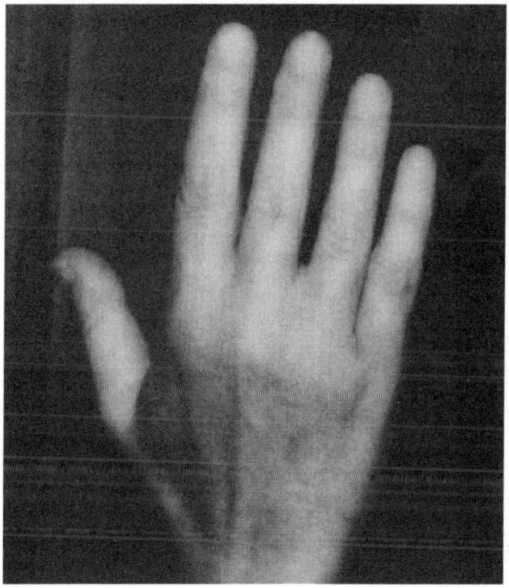

Picture 22

In the following Picture No. 23 we see prominent first fingers in both hands. In the right hand it is even longer than the middle finger, showing a domineering, inconsiderate, authoritarian personality. This finger rules over all the others. In the left hand we can also discern Hera in the matron aspect: independent, knowing her stature and capabilities in the world, as well as Zeus' leading role.

right *left*

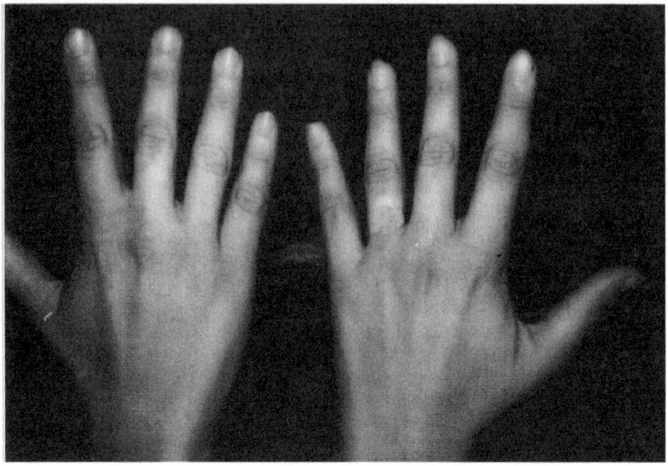

Picture 23

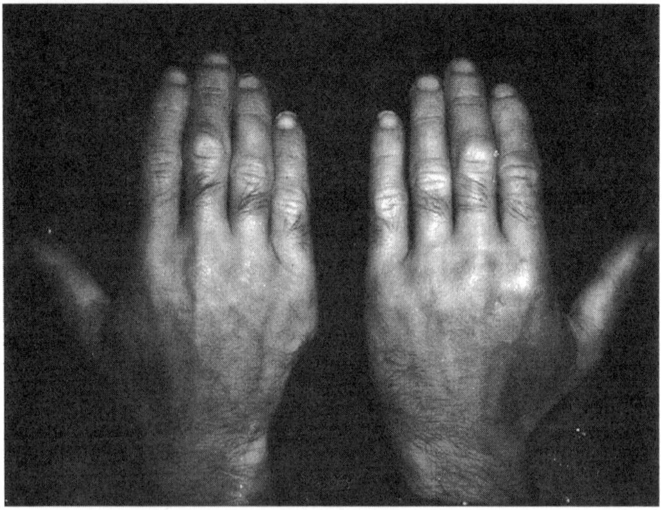

Picture 24: First finger "leaning" on and under second finger in both hands, showing feelings of inferiority. In the left hand also of resentment (see the difference in expression between right and left first finger).

The opposite – lack of self-confidence and self-assertion and feelings of interiority – will be seen when a well-structured finger of long or normal height ("normal" is when the finger reaches up and is a little above the middle part of the nail of the second finger) is bent in and its expression is weak. (Picture 24, in both left and right hands.)

Hestia: Another archetypal image is portrayed in this first finger in the form of Hestia, a feminine goddess, keeper of the hearth. She is the caretaker of the home, keeper of the fire, sustaining the family in the centre of the home, as a basis of structured society. Hestia, of the Goddesses, is the main one, as Zeus/Jupiter is for the Gods. "She is the source of all things, the paradox of human life."[1] Chirologically, we can say that Zeus, as father and husband signifies more the stand in the world outside, whereas Hestia, as mother and virgin, signifies the flame of the "inner world." She is a virgin who implies unfolding, becoming, the honorable, dignified aloneness of what one is. This is Hestia at her best. Originally she was much revered and her activities in the home – tending to the fire and cooking – were sacred. She is often anonymous and self-sacrificing, but nevertheless controlling. Her main characteristic is the ability to devote herself to the welfare of others up to being their victim, not being conscious that, in fact, she victimizes them through her sacrifices. She is a shadow figure to Hera but both show aspects of dominance, authority and control. Whereas Hera's activities are extroverted, turned outwards, to the world, Hestia's are inside, in the home, also to be understood in the symbolic "home" aspects of inner worthiness or unworthiness.

1. S.A. Demetrakopoulos, "Hestia, Goddess of the Hearth," *Spring 1979* (Texas: Spring Publications), pp. 55-73

Chirologically, Hestia's characteristics will be seen in the first finger tending towards the second finger, separated from the other fingers, yet expressive, portraying a Hestian aloneness and independence. Yet, when the finger is long and heavy or rigid and well apart from the other fingers, it would indicate the Hestian loneliness and dryness. An index finger conic in shape and tending towards the middle finger, while its first phalange, the one close to the palm, is longest, shows good cooking abilities and care for the house and children. The self-sacrifice of Hestia can also be seen in an index finger standing outward, or slightly bent in, away from the other fingers. It may indicate the self-sacrificing of inner development because of the duties of the home and dependents. If it is also short and heavy-looking, it also assumes Hestia's anonymity, hard toil and carrying the heavy burdens of the world in a self-sacrificing fashion. Hestia can also be seen in a man's hand as well as in a woman's hand.

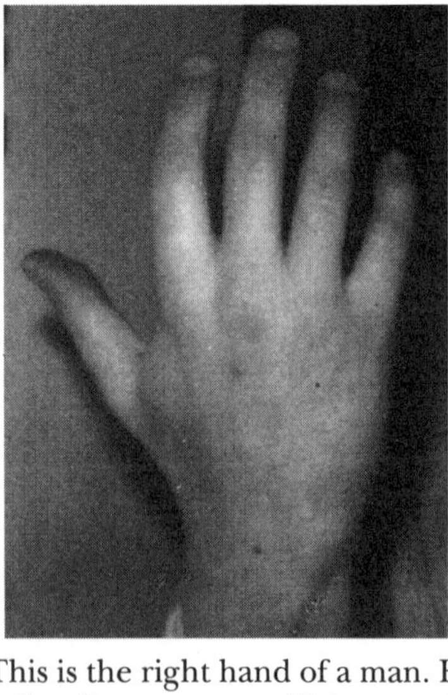

Picture 25: This is the right hand of a man. Hestia is portrayed in the first finger as a sacrificing, yet domineering figure. (Notice the thumb which is strong-looking.)

Here is an example of two pictures portraying Hestia in two different states. A widow, whose husband died of cancer, felt completely lost, since during their married life she had been constantly "tending the hearth." Subdued, anonymous, rejected as a woman, she came to the chirological test desperate about her potentialities. At that time she was trying to sort out her husband's business deals with his clients. Her index finger tended towards her middle finger and was under it. It was conic in shape and prominent. Being under the middle finger and tending towards it, expressed faithfulness, connectedness to the home, reliance on her thinking but with a feeling of inferiority. Other components in her hand showed that she was intelligent, capable of handling people and influencing them and with a very good commercial sense, which she was completely unaware of. She had practically no self-esteem which, of course, went back to her childhood and to her relationship to her parents. Her choice of a husband was in accordance with her psychic state. She was passive, closed off and nondescript, tending to the home and children, apart from her husband yet taking care of him, sacrificing, sad, separate and very lonely, all the Hestian characteristics. She never showed the jealousy and rage of Hera, the wronged wife, for instance. She accepted everything, yet never really gave of herself, remaining virginal.

Slowly, through therapy, her "Hestia" could realize her need for independence, for bringing out and living her other potentialities, for creating a home and for tending to the hearth of her inner world. She now heads her own office successfully and is highly appreciated. She has an open and warm home with children and friends; she chooses her relationships, lives alone but is not lonely.

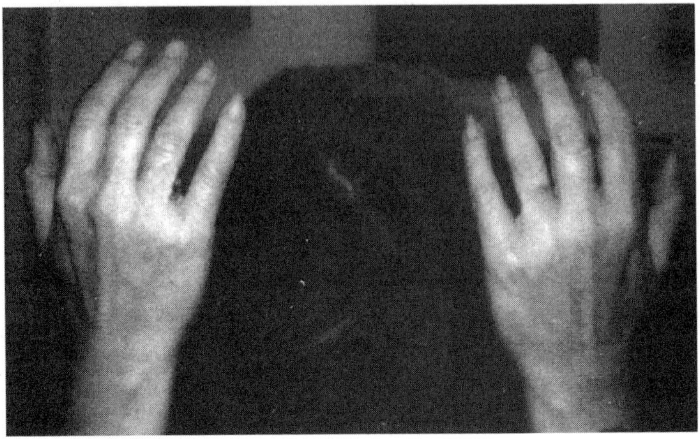

Picture 26: Hestia (first finger) bent in and a little under the middle finger.

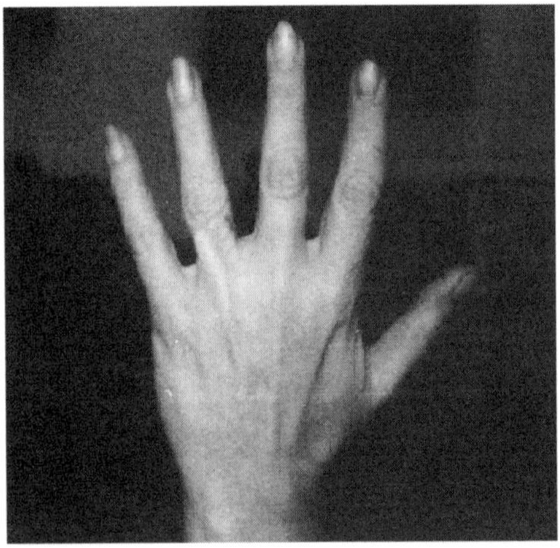

Picture 27: The inherent capability of an independent and developed Hestia.

Another example of different archetypal aspects of the first finger.

right *left*

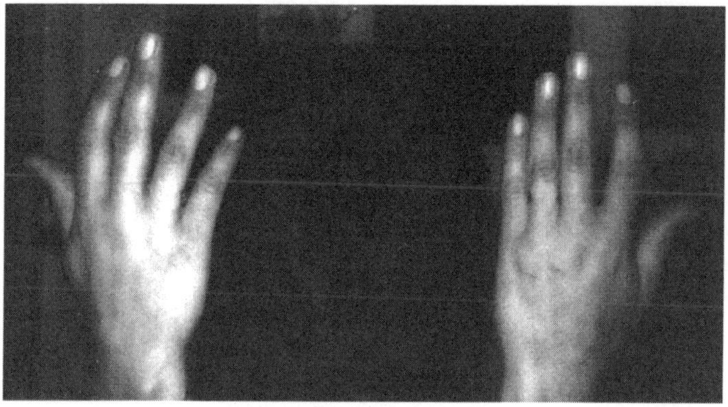

Picture 28. In the right hand, Hestia is in a sacrificing and dependent state, as well as Hera Chera, i.e., in her mourning state, the clinging yet rejected wife.
In the left hand, the first finger portrays lack of self-confidence – Hera in the maiden phase and Hestia in her sacrificing aspect, belittling herself. The finger does not stand upright.

Dreams about fingers, looked at chirologically, can at times serve as an additional way of interpreting the dream, as in the following example. A woman dreamt: "A snake bit my index finger."[1] Chirologically this could mean that a new awareness of her stand in the world – her Zeus, Hera or Hestia aspects – were becoming conscious.

1. Gustav Dreifuss, oral communication to the author, 1968

The middle finger – Saturn/Athena

The second finger, the middle finger, stands between Zeus and Apollo, between the "world" outside and the inner world. It is usually the longest finger in the hand and the stabilizer between these two aspects – the world of activity, consciousness and the world of feelings, evaluating, imagining, relating and intuiting. It stands between the conscious attitude and the unconscious urges and longings. In Freudian terms it also serves as the super ego. It shows our intellectual potentials, the kind of thinking – whether it is heavy, depressive, rigid, dull, or lively. It is important to note to which finger the middle finger tends, whether to Zeus or to Apollo. Tending towards Zeus would emphasize more the reality aspect, extraversion, outer world. Tending towards Apollo would mean more introversion and the influence of feelings and of the unconscious.

Saturn portrays both the Senex, the old man, and the Puer, the eternal youth, in all their facets. Athena, who sprang from Zeus' head, is the feminine goddess attached to this finger. Both Saturn and Athena represent forms of thought. Saturn emphasizes rules and regulations, restrictions and responsibilities, law and order and seriousness. He binds us to reality, to what "is." [1] In its negative form Saturn portrays dogmatism, negative thinking, narrow-mindedness, criticism, accusation, mental judgments, calcification, i.e., rigidity, and depression up to apathy. In alchemy Saturn symbolizes a dark, low, not yet thought-out content which must be brought into consciousness, the severed head. "Saturn is the head," as von Franz says.[2] In humanistic astrology[3] Saturn's function is the process

1. Hanni Binder, oral communication.
2. Marie-Louise von Franz, *An Introduction to the Interpretation of Fairy Tales* (New York: Spring Publications, 1970), p. 118
3. Michael R. Meyer, *A Handbook for the Humanistic Astrologer* (New York, Doubleday/Anchor Press, 1974), p. 75

of focalization and differentiation, growing to a sense of personal identity and security, but also inertia.

Chirologically, Saturn and Athena will be portrayed by a long, expressive, lively middle finger. In its softer-looking expression Athena will be more marked: in its stronger expression Saturn will be seen (see Picture 30).

Saturn in his Puer aspect is the eternal youth of aspirations and illusions, living in projections, opposing responsibility and retaining youthful folly at all costs. He lives with the possibilities still ahead, notwithstanding the reality of things as they are. He is the eternal optimist. There is always a spirit of freshness about him, whether in its positive or negative aspect.

The puer/puella aspect will be chirologically portrayed when the finger is slender and lively, with the upper phalange turning outward, together with some aspects that can be seen in the inner lines of the palm (Picture 29, in the left hand).

right *left*

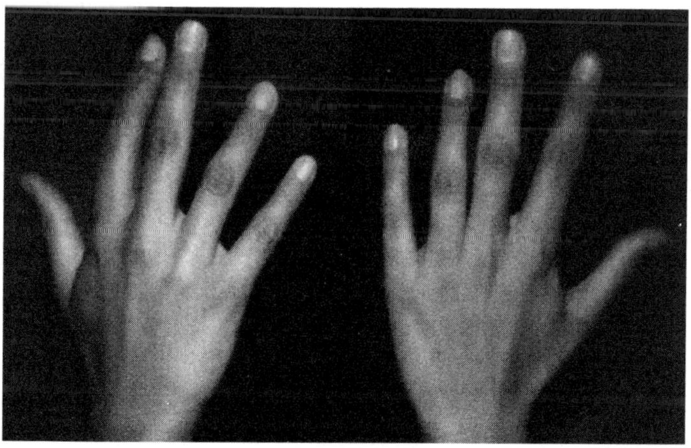

Picture 29. The Puer / Puella aspect of second finger.

right *left*

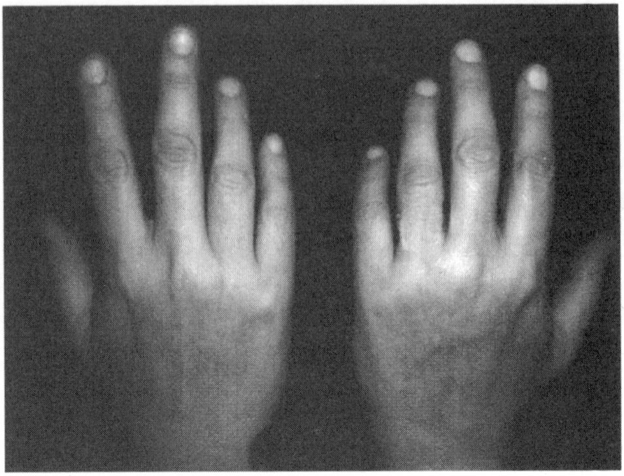

Picture 30. In this picture, the second finger of the right hand portrays Saturn dominating with rules and regulations. In the left hand this finger portrays Athena. It is softer-looking, even sad.

right *left*

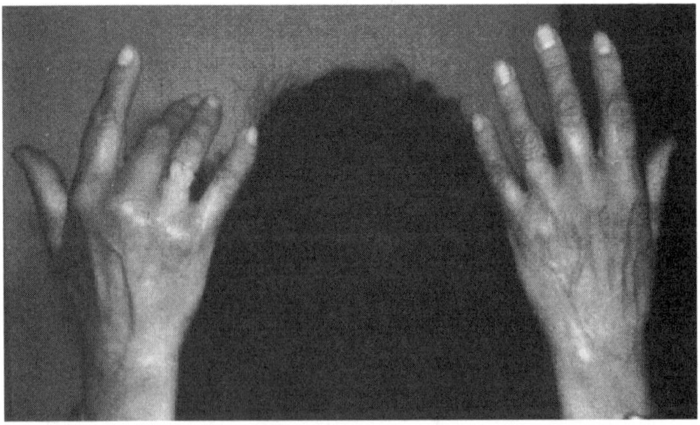

Picture 31

In his negative Senex aspect, Saturn is old, heavy, weary, pessimistic, rigid, stern, foreboding and limiting, opposing change. The middle finger turned inwards towards the palm, heavy and sad, portrays depression that is more anchored in negative thought patterns (Picture 31, in the right hand). In the same picture in the left hand, the second finger portrays Athena in her prime.

Athena, as feminine counterpart, is the advisor. Born out of Zeus' head, she belongs to the cerebral area: the middle finger is the "head" of our fingers. She is the father's daughter who, born without a mother, is connected wholly to him, in an ambivalent form. The myth does mention Metis as the mother of Athena, who, while pregnant, was swallowed by Zeus. With Hephaistos' help, Athena sprang out from Zeus' head. Metis means "mind," advice, practical insight, understanding and thinking through. From this we see that Athena's mother, too, is also all "head." Psychologically, this means that the mother of a woman who has a strong inner image of Athena may be intelligent, practical, rational and/or animus-possessed, i.e., full of ideas and opinionated, without warmth or softness.

The ambivalent relationship between daughter and father and her identification with him is her way of defending herself from the threatening masculine principle to her femininity. On the one hand she wants to be accepted and admired by her father. On the other hand she is always afraid of being "swallowed," so that, by identifying with the aggressor, she thinks she saves herself, but, in fact, loses her femininity. Athena is always alone yet a friend, who is always present in times of need for counselling and direction. According to myth, she is always present beside the hero, not in body but as an empowering presence. She is "as if" she were a man, "man-to-man," and a virgin. She is called Athena Pallas, meaning "maiden," or Athena Parthenon, meaning "virgin."[1] However, it is not the virginity of Hestia, nor that of Artemis. She is not anonymous or self-sacrificing, nor shy, nor alluring. She is practical, efficient, present in the here-and-now and complete. She has the ability to reflect and think things through. According to myth it was she who gave Perseus the mirror, to help him kill the Medusa – the devouring power of the feminine – the mirror representing the possibility of reflection.

In her negative form she represents animus possession, reflection turned into opinions. She becomes opinionated, harsh, judgemental and critical (Picture 32, right hand). But she is also known as Athena of the crafts and is endowed with technical abilities. Second finger upright and square in form shows this side of Athena (Picture 29, page 69 right hand, and in Picture 32):

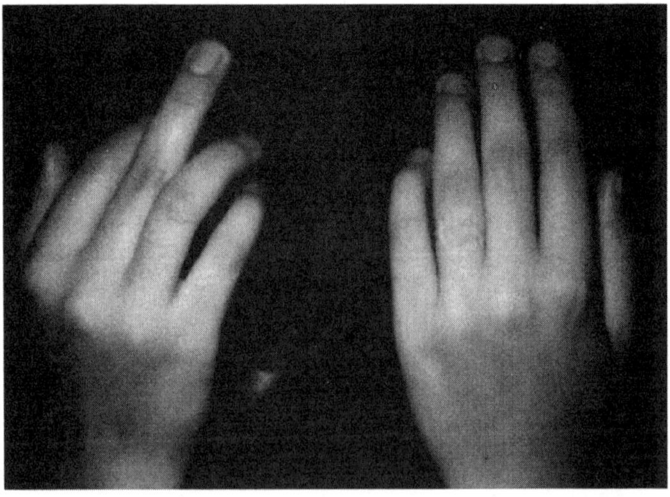

Picture 32 depicts Saturn in the right hand in its hardening facet, domineering and subduing the other fingers' capabilities. However, it can also pertain to Athena in her negative, animus-ridden, facet.

1. Karl Kérenyi, *Athena: Virgin and Mother* (Zurich: Spring Publications, 1978), p. 13

A woman whose "Athena" is dominant may learn to accept her aloneness – not loneliness – in a masculine world and use her reflecting ability. Athena is an inner image for most women of today. She occupies the middle and central part of our psyche but also of our hand, the middle finger being literally central. We are all daughters of the patriarchal culture and of the dominance of the masculine principle within. We belong to it so we tend to identify with it, becoming more "man" than "woman," victims of our animus, rational and intellectual – or simply animus-possessed. Or, we tend to feel very inferior and without value (Picture 33, especially in the left hand).

right *left*

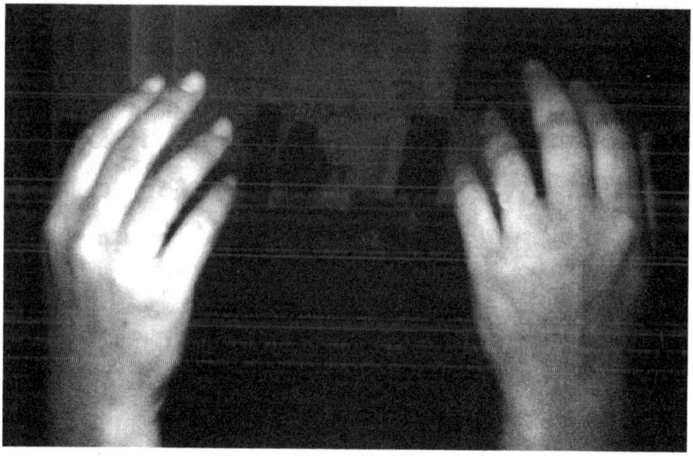

Picture 33. Notice the second finger in the left hand: though bent inward, it protudes more than the other fingers, showing negative thought forms.

I came to view both Saturn and Athena as the major archetype underlying superego aspects which result in problems with the body, especially eating disorders. While for men, Saturn's asthenic and rigid thought forms will be accentuated, for women, it will often be Athena's problems with the father imago. We are all very conscious of and engrossed in our bodies – in dieting, trying desperately to eliminate our fatness, become thin, airy, empty, hollow-bellied, in order to become an image, a presence felt but not touched, not realizing our value as daughters of our "fathers."

Hillman says of Athena: "She is the archetypal person within the fantasy of normality."[1] She is "the inner space-making function of mind. The Goddess who grants *topos,* judging where each event belongs in relation with all other events. She is mind as a containing receptacle which normalizes through interior organization."[2]

Dreams confirm chirological findings. However, chirology may often help to understand a dream. A woman dreamt that her middle finger was cut off.[3] Chirologically we could say that it might signify a possible break of the stabilizing function. In fact, the dream was a warning of a coming breakdown.

Here is another example of a dream: A woman dreamt that she and her lover were exchanging rings. He put one on her middle finger and she put one on his.[4] This dream points to their relationship, both on the outer-objective level and on her inner-subjective level. The relationship apparently, at that moment, does not lead to an outer marriage, as the ring given in the dream is not the usual wedding-ring and is not put on the third, "ring," finger. The bond between them belongs to the binding of second finger, Saturn and Athena.

1. James Hillman, "On the Necessity of Abnormal Psychology: Ananke and Athene," in *Facing the Gods* (Dallas: Spring Publications, 1980), p. 27
2. *Ibid.*, p. 29
3. Ken Newman, oral communication to the author, by permission, 1979
4. By permission of the dreamer.

Looking at the dream from this perspective, on the outer objective level, this can point to a relationship based on friendship, mutual responsibility, seriousness, stability and order, Saturn's and Athena's positive characteristics. It can also point to a binding of the puer side of the lover and/or the puella side of the woman. In other words, that they become aware of their projections, illusions and youthful folly, and yet retain the young spirit attached to it. On the subjective level, the dream points to a "coniunctio" on an inner archetypal level between her ego and her inner masculine side, binding Athena and Saturn, that is, to be more responsible to her Athenian and Saturnian characteristics in all of their aspects, including the ones mentioned above.

Third Finger – Apollo/Artemis-Persephone

We have dealt so far with the more cognitive, conscious side of our hand. The third finger brings us to the midst of our feeling values, inner life, our relationship to everything around us, our creative abilities and capabilities and a sense of form inherent in man, not belonging to the domain of will, rational thinking and ambition. It is the world of the muses, art, literature, poetry, music and inner expression.

The third finger portrays the weaving of visible and invisible threads of feeling values and judgments in our relationship to others and to ourselves, denoting them and us as worthy or unworthy, good-bad, wanted-unwanted, rejected, humiliated, adored and exalted, loved or unloved. It can show arrogance or hurt, shame and vanity, dependence or freedom. It can also convey egocentricity, narcissism, adventurousness, opportunism, and even gambling tendencies.

It is astonishing that the finger which usually shows, what I call the Son/Daughter psychology, with all its forms of bondedness mentioned above, is portrayed archetypally by both Apollo and his twin sister, Artemis, for they are the most free gods in the pantheon. Astrologically, Apollo corresponds to the Sun, which is associated with the heart and spine, with the source of will. It is not the will-power but the source of it – creativity and generosity; Sun as a potentiality. In humanistic astrology the Sun's function is sustainment, its process is purpose-giving and its purpose is integration.[1] Liz Greene says: "It reflects the individual's urge to become himself... what one is in potential, in essence."[2]

This, then, is the purpose of this finger: to bring us to our essence, out of captivity and towards the freedom that these archetypal figures represent. Apollo is cool, detached, lives by his own rules of feeling values. He is impersonal but has a clear "sight" into things. He has both an analytical ability and an intuitive insight. His oracle is fateful as it comes from irrational knowledge. He is the god of medicine, as healer and killer. He is the god of sudden death with his bow and arrow, never missing the target. His mother is Leto, a night-goddess.

According to legend, Apollo's birth is connected with suffering. Leto suffered for nine days and nine nights because Hera, who was jealous of her bearing a child of Zeus, kept Ilithyia, the Goddess of childbirth, from coming to Leto.[3] Every creativity apparently, true to the myth, has to suffer greatly before its birth. The story of the birth of Apollo, being the God of the Arts, portrays the process of creativity. It starts in the dark; it is difficult, long and full of suffering but it turns golden once it is born. Thus, Apollo by this story, is connected to suffering. Inner life, relationships, outwardly and inwardly, as well as the spiritual insights and clarity that hopefully ensue are all imbued with suffering. Suffering is their birthright. That is

1. Michael R. Meyer, *op. cit.*, p. 71
2. Liz Greene, *Relating* (London: Coventure, 1979), pp. 30-31
3. Karl Kérenyi, *The Gods of the Greeks* (London: Thames & Hudson, 1971), pp. 133-34

perhaps why so often this finger is attached to adjacent fingers or bent in and its expression is depressed. At times the only way out of suffering and captive states, be they inner or outer, is through being creative, or using the creative abilities residing in this finger.

Apollo's whole nature is said to be musical. It is the "music" in the art form that makes it art, thus transforming activities of different faculties into art. A third finger which is lively and expressive, helps transform the activities of man into "art," in no matter what type of activity be it the art of cooking, the art of speech, the art of writing or communication, or even the art of forming relationships and the art of healing.

In his "shadow" facet the golden Apollo can symbolize the glitter of superficiality, feeling values turn into sentimentality, pseudo-feeling values or too-strict feeling values. Being aloof and distant can turn into haughtiness, egocentricity and narcissism.

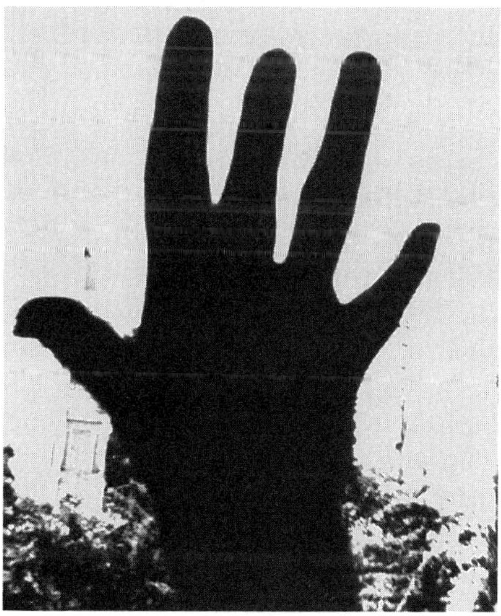

Picture 34

Picture 34 shows the hand of a woman with an abnormal structure of fingers, each one different in form. The second (Saturn/Athena) finger is abnormally short, connected to the first (Zeus/Hera) finger. This shows an inability to fulfill its task of stabilizing the personality, of being a responsible adult. She was tied to her ambitions (controlling Zeus/Hera). Yet her Apollo, third finger, is exceptionally expressive, well developed, long and free. She was a very special artist, a painter and a poet. Her Apollo was her inner physician. But it also shows Apollo's other, shadowy, traits. Further examples will be discussed in the samples of chirological consultations.

Artemis, or Diana, is the goddess of forests and animals, and of the hunt. She belongs to Nature. The forest can symbolize the entanglements of our inner life and the animals our connection to instinctuality, nature, animality and animation. Artemis, belonging to nature, portrays her ability to live naturally, dancing in inner and outer spaces. To be one with nature is to flow with the tides of nature, of birth and death, of ever-becoming, of process. In this respect she represents the possibility for transformation. She is the huntress, knowing her target and never missing it, like her brother Apollo. When chasing or being chased she is provocative, alluring and unreachable. She represents free, independent femininity, connected to nature, spaces, and dance. She animates all around her. Her function is "soul-making," to use Hillman's expression.[1] She is the goddess who assists at childbirth. According to myth, upon her birth she was the one to assist her mother in her delivery of Apollo, her twin. Artemis therefore represents the ability to assist at beginnings, in new births, as a midwife. Whereas Athena is a

1. For a fuller understanding of the term "soulmaking," see: Hillman, James, *Re-visioning Psychology* (New York: Harper and Row, Harper Colophon Books, 1975), pp. 167-193

presence assisting the hero in deeds and thoughts, Artemis assists in the act of creation. Yet she also kills instantly with her bow anyone who dares to trespass uninvited into her domain. Her opposite facets are negative feeling values, vindictiveness and cold and unrelated feeling judgements. As huntress she may be on the run, alert to possible assaults. Homer called her "a lioness unto women."[1] She never gives herself to anyone, not even to herself; she is both victim and victimizer, thus she becomes the victim of her own victimization. She can be bad, resentful, a killer.

I also designate Persephone to this finger as the daughter aspect to both parents.[2] She is the "shadow" figure of Artemis. She is never free but always captive, the eternal victim. She either belongs to mother or to father or to both the whole year round. She is a pleaser, a collaborator, never becoming rebellious (rebelliousness is more of an Artemisian trait). In her care for her mother, Demeter, she is in fact mothering the mother. This portrays the bonding of Mother/Daughter, also in relationships to men as husbands/fathers, serving them obediently, mothering them or, alternately, being their daughters. She is self-effacing in bondage, accepting fate with sadness or melancholy. Her sadness and depression is her expression of unexpressed rage. (Picture 35, in the right hand.)

Apollo and Artemis at their best can be seen when the third finger stands independently and is lively in expression.

An example comes to mind: A young woman came to a chirological test feeling depressed, although everything in her life was "objectively" fine. She had just married the

1. Paul Friedrich, *The Meaning of Aphrodite* (Chicago: University of Chicago Press, 1978), p. 85
2. Karl Kérenyi, *The Gods of the Greeks* (London: Thames and Hudson, 1974), pp. 232, 252

man she loved, held an important position in her work and was well-loved by those around her – yet she felt depressed. Her third finger was exceptionally fine and expressive and stood by itself. Her Artemis could not accept her being married and "bound." She felt fenced in and not free. The humdrum of everyday life and duties were not exciting or lively. Once she could disidentify herself from her Artemis, yet find a way to become aware of Artemis' needs in her, tending to them within marriage and reality, her depression was gone. She needed to give inner space to her soul in her life.

right *left*

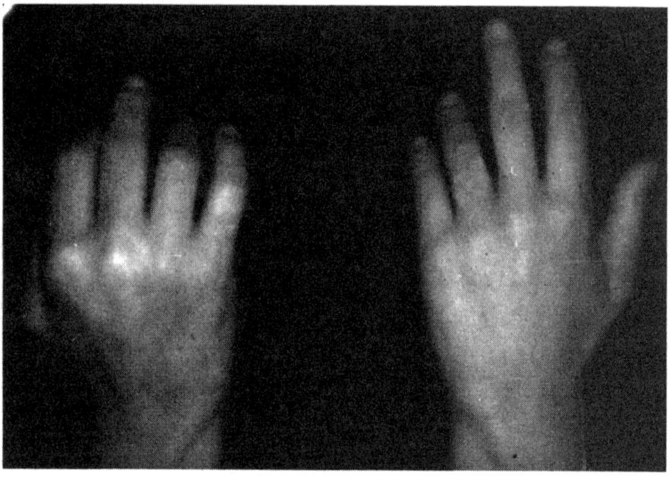

35. Third finger of right hand bent in, suppressed, subdued; second finger slightly bent but strong, showing negative thought forms (Saturn).

Again, differentiating between Apollo and Artemis causes a difficulty. Although being in many respects similar, Apollonian traits would be found more frequently in men than in women and Artemisian traits more frequently in women than in men. The third finger clinging to the second finger will show aspects of captivity, dependence and vulnerability. (Picture 36, a son/daughter's psychology, needing the father protection of Saturn's 'head' or the 'adult,' inwardly and outwardly.)

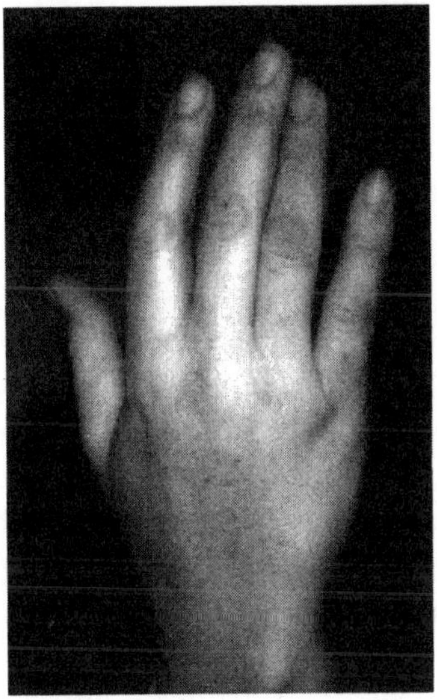

Picture 36

When the finger is bent in towards the palm and weak in expression, it signifies a state of depression connected to being a victim, a scapegoat, a prisoner of oneself or of circumstances. Both these last two states pertain also to the image of Persephone, both are forms of dependency as opposed to freedom.

A dream of a man in analysis:[1] "A blond girl and I provoke each other sexually. She bites my two middle fingers at the top phalanges of my left hand. I bite all her fingers. The bite is followed by a strong erotic sensation. I am afraid she is going to bite my other fingers and I escape. She beats me. I beat her cruelly, till she loses consciousness. I find refuge in a house where my parents

1. Permission granted for use here.

are and this gives me confidence. Nevertheless the terrible girl arrives and tries to get in with the aid of an enormous knife that sticks out of her. My father blocks her way at the door. I realize that this is not enough and succeed in getting the knife out of her hand. She runs away. I realize that it is impossible to repair my fingers back and I give medical interpretations as to why it cannot be done. I am glad I have medical knowledge to impress my parents."

The two middle fingers of the dreamer's left hand chirologically would point to second finger Saturn/Athena and third finger Apollo/Artemis. The feminine in this dream is threatening. In an erotic play the girl, an anima aspect of himself, eliminates or better, cuts the stabilizing faculty between the conscious and unconscious sides of his psyche, preventing the use of the rational thinking and adult reasoning ability. So, too, with his third finger Apollo/Artemis, the finger showing capabilities, artistic inclination and clear insight. These are also mutilated. Having been bitten at the top phalange shows that both of them pertain to the spiritual realm. This means that the damage was done to the spiritual abstract facets of his thinking and creative potentialities. He, on his part as the ego, mutilates his anima's capabilities in all her spheres – he bites all her fingers. The erotic excitation that accompanies this destructive, aggressive play shows the dreamer as being captive in his fear – aggression but at the same time is fascinated with the realm of the feminine which is so menacing. He regresses into the "son's" psychology, needing the father to save him. Only then can he disarm the feminine. She is gone but the damage is done. He retreats into intellectually acquired knowledge – the domain of the masculine – to impress his parents.

According to the analyst, this patient is in fact blocked in his dealings and in his work, both in the outer world and in his inner world. Engrossed in personal, material comfort, he is dependent upon his parents.

The goddesses are the different "anima" aspects or images of the masculine. They also represent different forms of femininity in women. There is not one kind of femininity. We usually distinguish femininity to imply softness, acceptance, relating, containing, caring, uterus-like confinement, passivity, or the opposite – its devouring and castrating, opinionated, even chaotic aspects.

When we look into the different images of the goddesses that are portrayed in our fingers – Hera, Hestia, Athena, Artemis and Persephone – we see that each one of them portrays a different kind of femininity, which is inherent in all of us. Yet they are alone and virginal. Somehow, the deepest aspects of femininity in all of us, women and men alike, are alone, are "just-so," they are what they are, complete unto themselves, yet also always becoming. They represent the possibility of the recurrent becoming of that which unfolds, true to its nature.

Understanding these distinctions and accepting and realizing their functions may help both men and women to know their inner counterparts and to find ways of living with them, because by falling into identification with the archetypes in an unconscious way our lives can be ruled and overpowered by them.

The Fourth Finger – Mercury/Hermes

The little finger is the most paradoxical and complicated of all the fingers as its name implies: Mercury/Hermes in all his guises and intricacies. He is the messenger of the gods, always on the road and at crossroads. God of thieves, he is quick, versatile, cunning and spirited. He has no feminine counterpart. He shows us the inner roads of our inter- and intra-relationships. Hermes, being a phallic god is connected with sexuality, which conveys our essence at the deepest level. In Hebrew, sexual union is expressed by the word "Yada" which means "knowing"; it is not an acquired knowledge, but an inward one. Our sexuality is deeply rooted to our essence and conveys it through its manifestation. To know the partner sexually in this respect, is to know his/her essence. It is a most intimate knowing, if we only allow it. López-Pedrazza, in a Hermes-like manner, says it a bit differently: "Our sexuality… marks the roads we tread in life like mile-stones. Thus our sexual images, fantasies, and imagination participate in the psychological commerce at the borderline of our psyche marking both the internal and external realms of life."[1] Hermes is the servant of the gods and as their messenger he is "on the go," on the way, always connecting. He is *enodios,* ("by the road") and *hodios* ("belonging to a journey"). He is in charge of all forms of communication and is the prototype of the trickster, tricking us into experiencing life and its havocs. He can trigger us into becoming conscious or lure us into unconsciousness and deceit. He is the energy behind transformation, namely in the process. As Lord of the Road he is also known as Lord of the soul, the soul on its never-ending road. As Mercury, he personifies the mercurial child, the psychopomp aspect, being everywhere and holding the soul's process on the road to its task.

Chirologically, this finger serves as the trigger which allows us to utilize all of our capabilities, like the sperm which activates life, or like the ignition of a car which starts the motor going. It shows us how we communicate in all spheres of life, be it sexually, verbally, socially or academically. It also shows scientific and commercial abilities as well as resourcefulness (Picture 37).

Hermes, being the guide of the soul in the intricacies of life, serves as protector in contrast to Saturn whose role is that of controller and judge. Hermes represents the inner child whose vulnerability to hurt, pain, rejection and abandonment makes him learn to react as protection. He paves our way, either by closing off or rejecting

1. Rafael López-Pedraza, *Hermes and his Children,* (Einsiedeln: Daimon Verlag, 1989, p. 15)

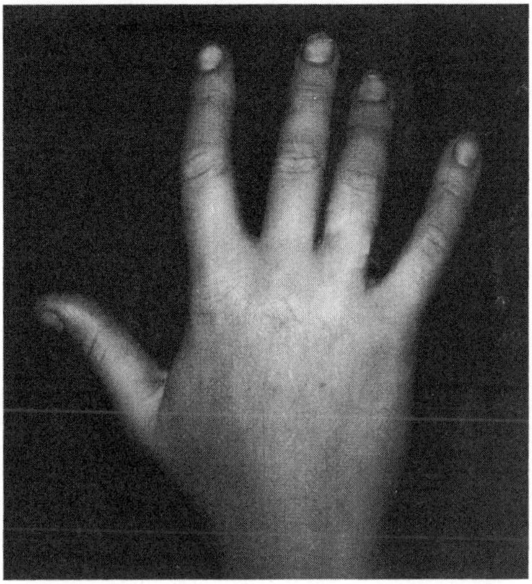

Picture 37. Fourth finger resourceful and alive

right *left*

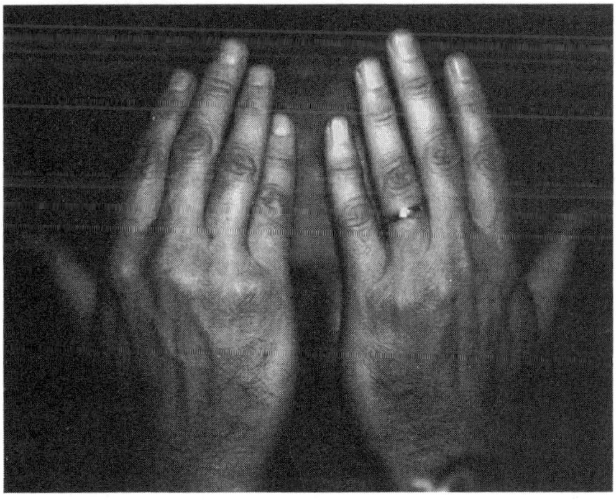

Picture 38. Fourth finger in left hand long, expressive, alive, sensitive. This is how the person communicates in his interrelationships, as well as the way he utilizes his other capabilities. It portrays verbal and scientific abilities.

others (when the finger is far away from the other fingers), distrusting, despairing, or with cunning and resourcefulness, independently and freely (Picture 37, right hand); or he can just be very correct in all his ways (Picture 38, also right hand).

Being smaller than the other fingers, it "serves" them as it leads or leads away the capabilities and characteristics portrayed by the other fingers. It is closely connected to Apollo, the third finger. According to myth, Hermes gave Apollo the lyre. Hermes has the instrument, the lyre, that makes the "music," the sound, the tone of how we communicate our abilities whether in the arts (acting, painting or writing), or in business acumen and commerce (upright or crooked, honestly or dishonestly); also in sex (freely or fearfully, ashamed, inhibited, rejected, unwanted). These are the "tones" that form our communications in all types of relationships. Especially our inter-relationships depend basically on the activity, forcefulness and resourcefulness of our Hermes. Intimacy – "into-me-see"[1] can be achieved only when our mercurial child and his vulnerability are present and real relationship formed when both partners can allow their hurt and painful child be included and accepted by the other.[2] This can only be developed when our inner vulnerable "child" aspect, together with the vulnerability of our inner "son/daughter" aspect (expressed in the third finger), feels safe to be included. There is always a hidden desire or even need for the feeling of "magic" in relationships. Often this "magical touch" disappears when our weakness and vulnerability is manifested and an interesting pattern develops. When our vulnerabilities – but not our partner's – are

1. I thank Arthur Levy for this phrase
2. I am indebted to the teaching of Hal Stone and Sidra Winkelman in *Embracing Each Other* (San Rafael, Calif.: New World Library, 1989)

included in the relationship, the magic is there too; magic as another synonym for projection. Magic is then turned into projection and we expect that our partner will "magically" be all that we have missed in our childhood, in our life up to now, the "messiah" who will heal our wounds.

What is in fact "magical" in this respect? It is the mercurial unpredictability. It is the ever-possible change, the unexpected probabilities, the ever-new becoming. Stretching it further we can say that, once we allow our vulnerable "child and son/daughter" to be accepted within a relationship without projecting the yearning for a magical outsider, i.e., a partner, to fulfill our needs and heal our wounds, this magical child, residing dormant, can become alive, turning our relationships into a vibrating venture of ever-new ways and possibilities.

Hermes gives rhetoric ability to Saturn's orders and laws. It can also lead away or into some of the depression belonging to Saturn. It may give eloquence to authoritative Zeus and also cunning and resourcefulness in dealing with the world.

The fourth finger's position in the hand and its relationship to the other fingers and especially its expression, will convey its influence and guidance in our personality. In Picture 39, we can see the fourth finger in the left hand developed, expressive and long. The upper phalange turns to the outside, showing curiosity (also in sex), and versatility: also eloquence in all forms of communication, be it in speech or art (Apollo/Artemis finger free and expressive). In the right hand the fourth finger shows reticence and compliance.

right *left*

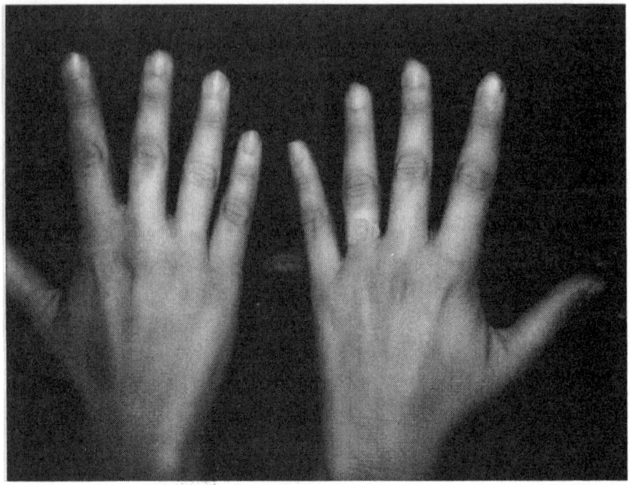

Picture 39. In this picture Hermes is a helpful guide, as compared to the fourth finger in Picture 40.

right *left*

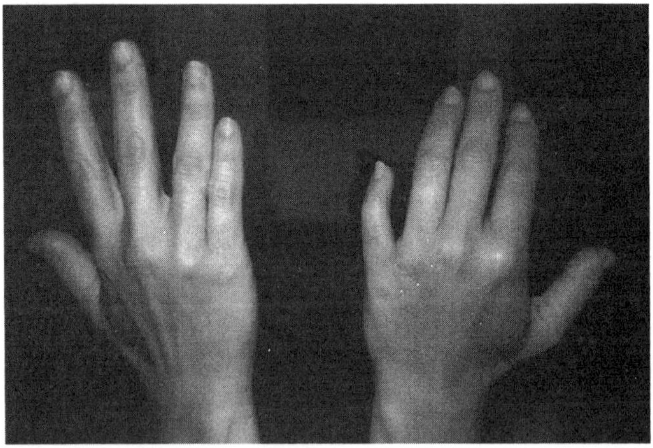

Picture 40. In the left hand the fourth finger is low-set, away from the other fingers and very small in size, indicating a childish, tricksterish Mercury/Hermes, not in alli-

> ance with the other components of the personality. In the right hand, though, the fourth finger is close to the third, complying and connected to it, meaning that Hermes as the child aspect as well as his way of communication is bonded to and dependent upon Apollo, i.e., upon feeling values and judgments. Notice also the severe expression of the second finger, Saturn.

A crooked fourth finger shows a tendency to conceal, to lie, to trick (see Pictures 40 and 41, left hand, fourth finger). It should be mentioned that we have to verify this trait by looking into the lines in the inner palm.

right *left*

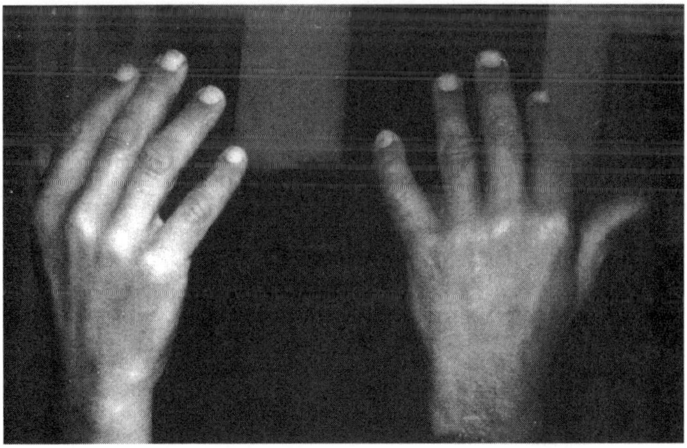

Picture 41

right *left*

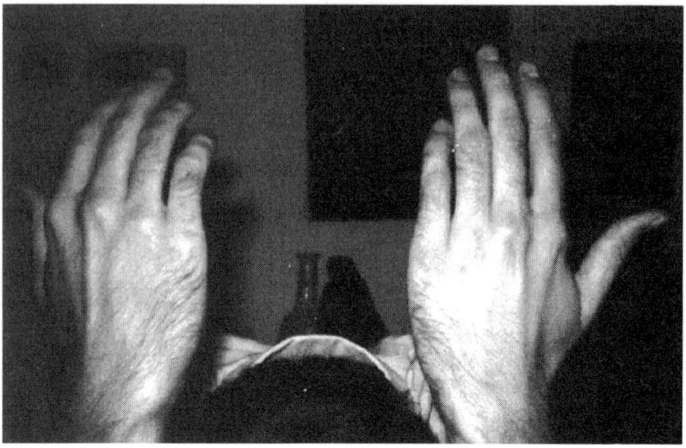

Picture 42. Present psychic state: In the left hand: A shy, dependent "child" afraid, "needing" protection of the son's role as well as other Apollonian traits.

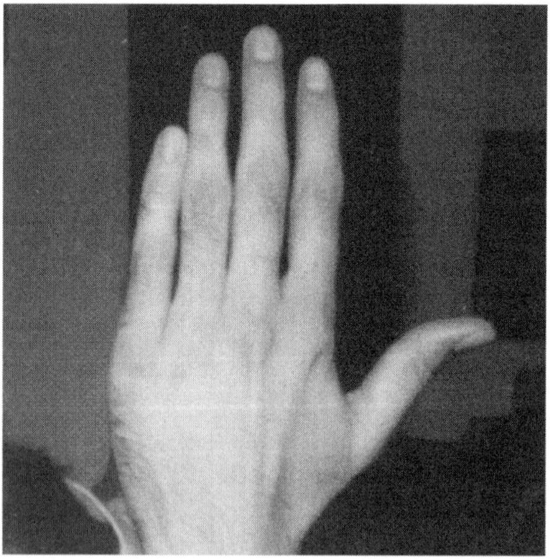

Picture 43. The inherent expression and form: a lively well-developed fourth finger yet not free to express itself fully, still dependent, and very correct and obedient.

Summary

Looking from this perspective, we can see how the fingers portray the whole gamut of complementary energy patterns. Our stand in the world, our inferiority or superiority, our self-assertion, self-esteem or lack of it, all are expressed by our first finger. Our patterns of thought, our assumptions, opinions, criticism, and the qualities of our thinking – deep, shallow, practical, etc. – are expressed in the second, middle finger. Feeling values, judgements and artistic capabilities are revealed in the third finger. Sexuality, agility, spiritedness, as well as all forms and capacities of communication, are expressed and conveyed in the fourth finger.

Fingers need space between each other. Not too much, but space enough to be able to relate independently to each other. Space allows the interplay of relationships of parts within a whole. When fingers lean on or hide behind another finger, there is no "space" for relating, there is dependency or negation of the finger's characteristics by another characteristic portrayed by the other finger.

Fingers held tight to each other show closure, dependency and even apprehension to opening up. Likewise, spread-out fingers, with a more or less even space between them, show independence.

The Thumb

Last, but not least, we come to the thumb. Traditionally there is no name of a god attached to the thumb. It stands alone, separate from the other fingers but it is able to face each one of them. Its normal height is usually up to the middle of the first phalange of the first finger. Symbolically it shows that the function of the ego is in the reality sphere of our basic senses and needs, of things as they are. Another equation is with the fourth finger. Together with the fourth finger it symbolizes the "octave" of our personality, so to speak. It portrays, as mentioned before, the ego capabilities. The ego is the carrier of consciousness turned into action. The ego is the carrier, so to speak, of what we do with our consciousness: how we face and encounter the archetypal images and energies operating in our lives.

The form, height and expression as well as the angle between the thumb and the fingers and palm, will determine the ego's functioning. The angle conveys modes of activity. When the angle is at about 45 degrees from the palm it shows an ability to be active and independent in all ego-functioning. Closer to the palm conveys stricture up to passivity and the farther away from the palm shows modes of rebelliousness. It can often be found in the hands of adolescents: they need to be ego-minded. It is important to assess the thumb's expression and quality, i.e., potentiality. By potentiality I mean its degree of ability to differentiate, to evaluate, to suffer frustrations or persevere.

The expression will indicate how these aspects operate within us at the present moment; either not at all, rigidly, weakly or strongly or in a lively way. Together these will indicate the amount and the particular personalistic dynamic way the ego in its volition and execution, and the reflection attached to it, work.

A bent thumb with a weak expression will show fear of defeat and passivity. The higher the potentiality of the thumb, the more developed the person is. As was proved by the research in the hospital, the potentiality of the thumb serves as an indicator of the severity of pathology.

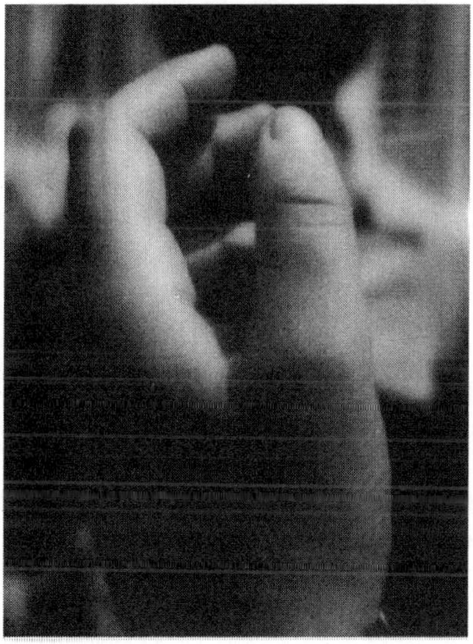

Picture 44. This thumb is weak in expression and potentiality

right *left*

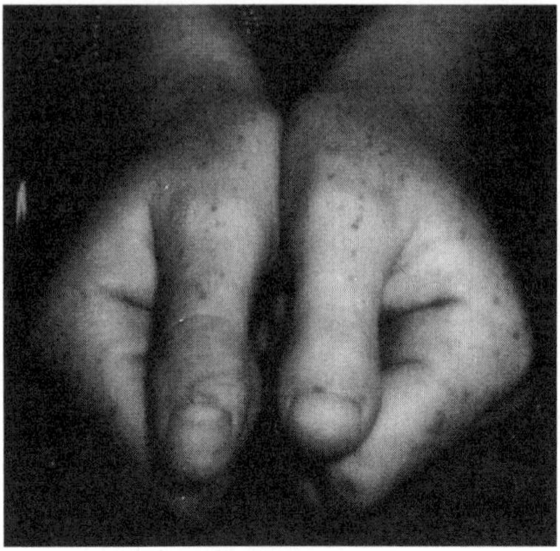

Picture 45. Right thumb: medium potentiality, lively expression. At the top it is conic in form. Left thumb: also of medium potentiality, rigid expression. Compare with picture 46 where both thumbs are of good potentiality and lively expression:

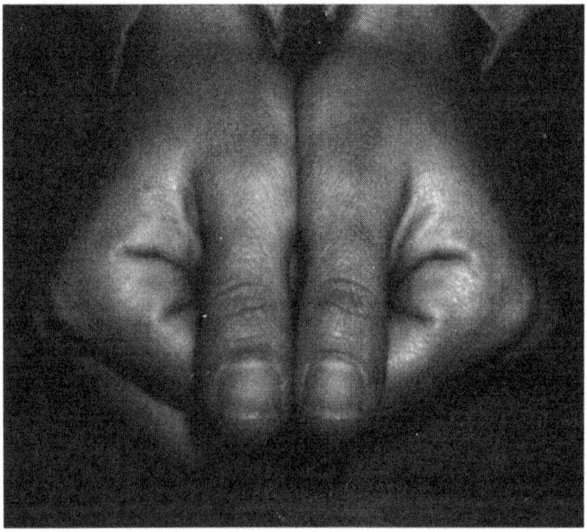

Picture 46

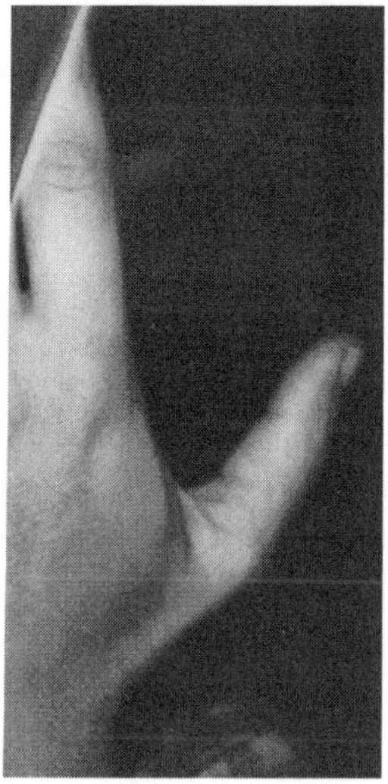

Picture 47 shows a well-developed, but rigid and passive thumb.

right *left*

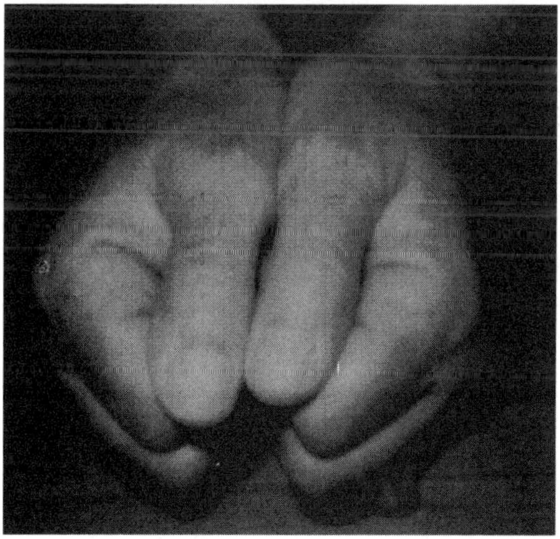

Picture 48. Both thumb of good potentiality, left thumb dependent on right thumb.

The higher the potentiality, the better our ability to react appropriately and accept our "pathologies," our soul's sufferings and pains. Hillman's[1] use of the phrase "pathologizing psychologically" is "to find a place for it, a way of accepting it, in general and as a whole... to know what it might be saying about the soul and what the soul might be saying by means of it."

The "low" position of the thumb with regard to the other fingers enables us to hold, for instance, the pen one writes with. It is in the hollow space between the thumb and the fingers, between "I" and the gods, that things get done. Only by counteracting, relating, encountering the "me" with the "not-me," the "I" with the archetype that manifests in my being, the "persons" living in my abode, can I discriminate, insight, understand, take a stand or run away, be overpowered, be rigid, or numb. A too-strong thumb, as an example, could bring about an inflation of the ego. Metaphorically, being "low" and smaller than the other three fingers (except the fourth finger) is to keep low and humble, and human.

1. James Hillman, *Re-visioning Psychology, op. cit.*, p. 57

e) The Archetypal Meaning of Mounts and Lines

Having given an overview of the archetypal layout, as portrayed by the fingers, we can now move to the mounts and the lines in the inner palm of the hand. The *mounts* under the fingers, at the distal part of the palm, are the manifestations of these archetypal images. The *lines* in the inner palms are the manifestations of the energies portrayed in the fingers and, as such, are energy conductors. They show the dynamics operating within the personality, transforming the archetypal images into soul. The vicissitudes of our inner battles, conflicts, suffering, ways of relating, feelings and thoughts – in short, our soul's voices, our cries and longings – find their expression here. In the interior, moist side of the palms, our "ground," the whole drama, already envisioned in the fingers, unfolds. There are three to four main lines and auxiliary and secondary lines, which are the dynamic connections between the main lines and which indicate inner activities and the markings of our life experiences. Like the blood vessels, they give life, warmth and color to our inner palm.

The main lines are: the thenar line, called the *life line;* the lower traverse line, called the *head line* and the upper traverse line, called the *heart line.* (All are formed already in the embryo on about the 55th, 65th and 80th days respectively.) I shall deal with each one of them in combination with the mounts as they pertain to them, also according to locality.

The mounts at the base of the palm and in its sides portray different archetypal images to those in the fingers. They are the following: In the radial part of the palm, at the base of the thumb, we have the *thenar mount,* called the mount of Venus or Aphrodite. I find Dionysus there, too.

Chirologically, the thenar mount portrays the vitality of the personality, its life force and instincts – the love of

General Map of the Characteristics portrayed in the Fingers and Mounts

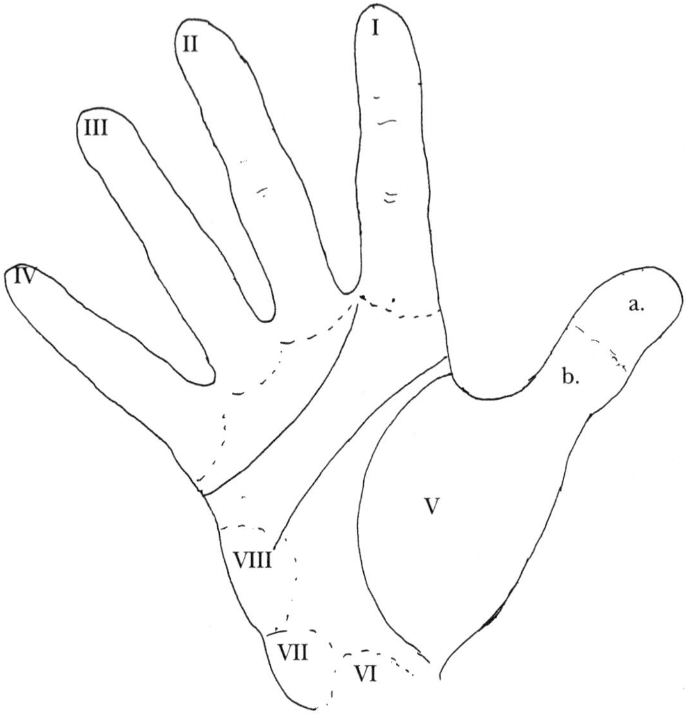

I Our stand in the world, our senses=organization, perception, etc. Representing the couple, patriarchal/matriarchal psychology: Zeus/Hera.
II Forms of thought. Super-ego, responsibility, seriousness. Representing the adult psychology: Saturn/Athena.
III Feeling values, relations, capabilities in art and medicine. Representing son/daughter psychology: Apollo/Artemis.
IV All forms of communication, inter-relationships, commerce, science. Representing the trickster and child psychology: Hermes.
V Vitality, life force, enthusiasm, joy: Aphrodite/Dionysus.
VI Unconscious inner knowledge, intuition, para-psi abilities, delusions: Neptune/Hades.
VII Unconsciousness, fantasy, imagination, source of creativity, dark night of the soul: Luna.
VIII Fighting abilities, force, aggression, resiliency: Mars.
Thumb: a. Will power, power of execution, ego capabilities
b. The thought attached to it.

The horizontal division of the palm and the main lines

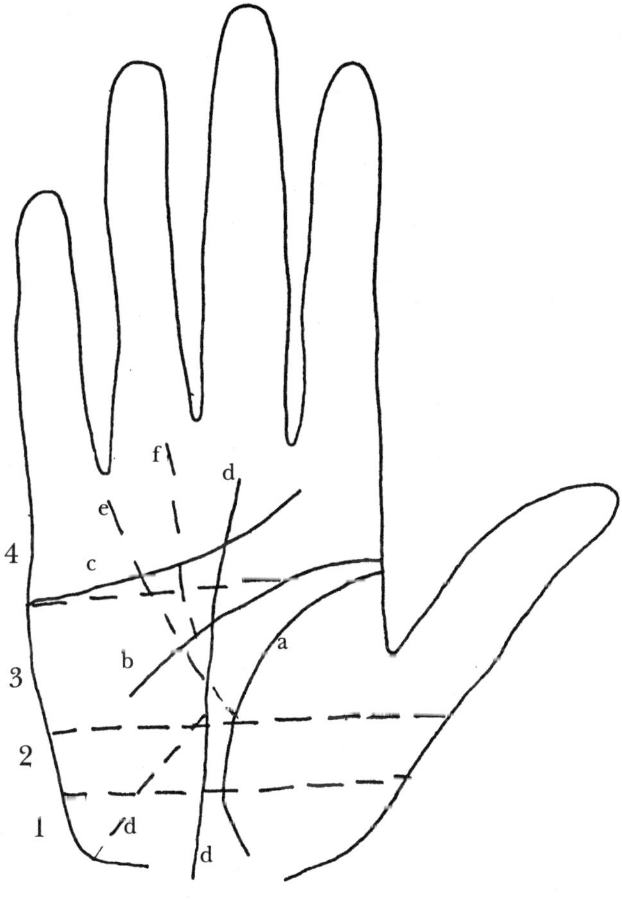

Lines: a. Vitality – life line
b. Lower traverse line – head line
c. Upper traverse line – heart line
d. Stabilizing-fate-line. Line of adaptation
e. Developmental line (mercurial line)
f. Intuition

1) deep unconscious, collective unconscious
2) personal unconscious
3) reality aspect
4) inter-/intra-relationships, feeling values, interests and capabilities.

nature, animals, children and mankind in general. So love in this respect is a synonym for vitality. It is a fact that when we are in love we are full of vitality; it is a life-giving force.

Aphrodite is the goddess of love in all its forms, from the most base to the most sublime. In Homer and Sappho she was the patroness of marital love (if you remember, her position in the hand is opposite to the first finger, representing the couple in marriage). She gives herself indiscriminately to anyone who wants her love and is completely amoral. She symbolizes growth, fertility and procreation; Euripides mentions her cosmic generative force and she is a lover of nature and of children. She is the most motherly of the goddesses, willing also to suffer for her child or lover and therefore she combines both eroticism and maternity[1]. Friedrich[2] mentions Anna Karenina as a prototype of this Aphrodite conflict – women who feel deep motherliness towards their children, yet have passionate extramarital affairs, or men who separate love from marriage.

Dionysus is the god of ecstasy and rapture, joy and madness, intoxication and sensuality. Together with Aphrodite, he represents lust in its physical, sexual form. A very pronounced lower mount will portray this state; but they also symbolize love in its depths and heights of mystical union. When the mount is more pronounced in the middle area, or a little higher, it shows a more sublime sexuality, that is one associated with Eros, love and care. Dionysus personifies on the one hand oblivion and drunkenness, and on the other, the spiritual, mystical experience of the senses. This brings to mind the connection between addictions and spirituality, one is the "shad-

1. Paul Friedrich, *The Meaning of Aphrodite* (Chicago: University of Chicago Press, 1978), p. 150
2. *ibid.*, p. 181ff

ow" of the other. Dionysus unites heaven and earth with the zest of the life force – a highly religious, mystical union, a freeing energy or an ecstatic state of being. He is closely connected to nature and its unpredictability, therefore he is very irrational. Both Aphrodite and Dionysus represent basic survival instincts. Their position opposite Zeus/Hera and Hestia points to their fundamental connection. Our survival instincts influence, and are influenced by, our stand in the world. We have here opposites drawn to extremes. Order, organization, and authority versus disorder, oblivion and chaos; institutional religiosity (Zeus) versus mystical and individual religiosity (Dionysus). When joined negatively with Dionysus, Zeus' love for conquest and patriarchal power can cause a person to become inflated or omnipotent to the point of mania. Hera's hatred joined negatively with Aphrodite sucks out the vitality and zest for life from a person caught in her frenzied jealousy, mad with the lust for power. Aphrodite and Dionysus, operating negatively, can usurp our social, educational and organized behavior patterns and bring anarchy and the collapse of all familial and social institutions as the ordered continuum of society. Joined positively, our stand in the world and our dealings with it, can be filled with Dionysus' enthusiasm and Aphrodite's love and care. Dionysus, according to myth, was a very loyal and loving husband to Ariadne; this in complete opposition to Zeus' infidelities. Having both opposites in the same part of the hand, including the thumb, confirms, physically speaking, the proximity of being able to be, in this instance, a Zeus, as an inner figure, loyal and loving, not only to others in his function as patriarch, but towards a wife, outwardly and inwardly. (This can add love and passion to marriage.) Our love-giving may be chosen more by an aware ego (thumb), rather than by our needs, be they conquest, possession, domination, vindictiveness, or fear of abandonment, rejection and illusory self-esteem.

Our Dionysian strivings, our longing to 'let go,' can be supported by our inner collective part – Zeus and Hera – and not thereby be annihilated. On the contrary, a validation of existence can be gained. One does not have to go mad and out of society in order to 'be.' We are often so afraid to 'be.' Being and its ecstasies are Dionysian in nature.

Dionysus, again according to myth, occupies in Olympus the same seat with Hestia, who gave her place to Dionysus. What does this imply? In Africa, a seat is an energy conveyor. Anyone sitting on the seat of a certain person receives his energy. That is why they maintain the House of Seats for storing the seats of deceased people who had specific duties in the tribe. The seats are never left standing straight, but are always tilted to the side, so that no passing soul's energy can use the seat before a new man has been chosen for the function. Hestia giving her seat to Dionysus would therefore imply that their energies are interchangeable.

Hestia, in our society, is dethroned, i.e., is split from her opposites as portrayed in the hand. In other words, still for a lot of men and women, the chores of the home are felt as burdens. At the most, they are carried out without love or joy. Lately, it must be said, a shift has been felt: it is "in" to be home and to tend the hearth. A Dionysian enthusiasm can give a spark of life to Hestia's role or anonymity and drudgery, elevating her vocation to an honorable one.

Surrounding the thenar mount, starting at the base of the palm and ending above the thumb, lies the thenar line, the *life line.* Like the mount this also shows the vitality and life-force of the personality, the physical-psychical temperament. When it forms a more or less closed circle around the thumb, it shows a possibility for centeredness or feeling "at-one-ment" and an ability to generate love and give to others. This circle was called by Dr. Debrunner, "the sun in our palm."[1] The two hand prints together form around the thumbs in the respective life- lines, a full sun as the centre of our consciousness, our ego. It is not a dispersed vitality energy. When the line tends more towards the centre of the palm or even towards the ulnar mount, it may, however, show a tendency to disperse (manifesting Dionysus in his lack of boundaries). When it starts not at the bottom but somewhere towards the middle, this usually shows that in the beginning of life, in childhood, the personal vitality and life force, were not available to this child. It emphasizes the lack of borders in the basic formation of our development. If it does not have this safety of "temenos" (or enclosure), it can be overflooded by fears of engulfment, of dispersion, of being abandoned. (We shall come back to this later). It is important to have secondary and auxiliary lines in the thenar mount as they portray the amount of activity of these instinctual energies, as well as the generating life force – especially when lines stretch out of the life line towards the middle and the distal parts of the palm in an orderly direction.

It is of interest that the lines of fear and courage are to be found in the thenar mount. In the book, *A Course in Miracles,*[2] it is said that the opposite of love is fear. I have often wondered about that, but it is true that when we fear, love disappears. Deep love protects us and those we love. Aphrodite is fearless. Often love gives us courage but courage without fear, on the other hand, is no courage, it is simply audacity and at times reckless risk-taking. Real courage is the overcoming of fear or, to put it another

1. Hugo Debrunner, oral communication to the author, 1964
2. *A Course in Miracles* (Tiburon, Calif.: Foundation for Inner Peace, 1975, 1985)

way, acknowledging fear. The fear lines are usually at the base of the mount up to the middle and the courage line is at the top of the mount, parallel to the thenar line, and is quite short. It begins somewhere between the edge of the thumb and the life line. We can say that courage "lies" between our sense of vitality, our will power and our ability to execute. The upper part of the thenar mount shows the ability to sublimate. This raises a pertinent question: Can we really be courageous once we sublimate our Dionysian life-force, enthusiasm and zest? Or is there an error in our interpretation of sublimation? By sublimation we usually mean suppression or transmutation of primary instinctual energies.

Sublimation comes from the word "sublime," which means lofty or exalted – that is, raised to a higher state, not suppressed or transmuted but simply honored. Courage is the hero's way. Location in the mount of Aphrodite and Dionysus points to both these energies being present in order to nourish the hero. He draws his courage from them and elevates them, that is by honoring them and acknowledging their fearfulness. So, courage is the connecting element between fear and love. The courage to love despite our fears or, better, with our fears, is to honor life and love.

We may find another line, called the self-destructive line, coming out of the upper thenar life line into the mount; it may be short or long and may be there together with the courage line, or without it. Having this line in the mount of Aphrodite/Dionysus shows how self-destruction is so intimately connected to courage, love, joy and the zest for life. In their names self-destruction often occurs, when negatively interpreted. Often, it is not lack of love which is the cause of self-destruction, it is *for* love, wrongly assessed. Being under the first (Zeus/Hera) finger, portrays how self-destructive can be our pride, ambition, quest for worldly gains and dominance; how it can curb our vitality, sensuality, and the ability to give and be in love. I have seen this line in the hands of very young children and in adults after years of analysis, and I also wonder if it may be a reminder of the ever-present inclination for self-destructiveness that many of us have. Women and men may be caught in hatred of their bodies, which is another form of self-destruction resulting in being under the spell of the negative aspects of Aphrodite and Dionysus.

In the middle zone between the thenar and ulnar side, opposite the middle and third fingers (Saturn/Athena and Apollo/Artemis), we have Neptune, god of the ocean, and Hades, god of the underworld. Neptune represents the depths of the sea and its contents, i.e., the depths of the unconscious where knowledge is not to be learned – it is there to be revealed. According to dictum, the unconscious knows more than we do. It is deep, always flowing, and fierce. Like the sea, it is irrational, unlimited, eternal; there are unfathomable riches in its depths. Yet, in its negative aspect, it can cause disruption of our thinking faculties and feeling values. It can drown us, overpower us, flood us with delusions and catastrophic intuitions, sweeping us into unconsciousness, as we shall see in the examples.

Hades can be looked at as the shadow of Neptune. He is considered to be one with Dionysus as death, and is another facet of unconsciousness. This is the underworld, where all demons abide and represents the hell we find ourselves in and, in its extreme form, it represents death. Situated in the middle proximal part of the palm, the mount of Neptune/Hades has a central position, just as the middle finger usually has a central position in the fingers, being the longest. Chirologically, this mount portrays inner stirrings of the deep unconscious, illusions and delusions, especially when many intersecting lines occupy this mount and its neighboring mounts. It also shows Psi abilities, inner knowledge, or wisdom.

Here, too, in this central place we find opposites drawn to extremes: rational thinking (Saturn/Athena) opposite irrational intuition and knowledge (Neptune/Hades). These extremes are usually quite split. However, situated, chirologically, on one continuum, they belong together. Their complementariness may point to a new way of thinking and a structuring to visions, adding other dimensions to our ordinary ways of thought-patterns.

Rising from the mount of Neptune/Hades and close to the life line, stems the *line of adaptation* also the *milieu line.* The line of adaptation, which is called the *fate line,* may not be there at birth – it can be formed later in life. This line can run up towards the middle finger or stem from the ulnar, Luna, mount. I also call this line the mediating and stabilizing line as it belongs to the second finger, Saturn/Athena. It shows the way we adapt or stabilize ourselves, the way we mediate between the unconscious and conscious parts of our psyche, how we steer our lives in these two realms, following the individualistic or collective way. Closer to the thenar life line, it will show a need for a collective way of belonging; the closer the line is to the thenar line, the closer the need for the home. Being away from the thenar line shows the urge to bring into consciousness and to the world the contents of our unconscious in an individualistic way.

The milieu (familial) line is quite short and is usually between the thenar line and the adaptation line. It may at times be instead of the missing thenar line, showing that – very early in life – the person was in symbiosis with one or both of the parental figures, being identified with them. This shows basic problems of identity, "auxiliary ego" and/or false-self. It emphasizes the traumas of the milieu on the developing child. It is interesting to note here that both these lines – the milieu and the stabilizing line of adaptation – stem from this central mount, as if to show us that the most important influences in our childhood and the way we steer our lives, are anchored in the innermost regions of unconscious knowledge and wisdom: in the extra-sensory realm. They can direct us through inner listening and connectedness to their deep insights and the sixth sense, the seat of intuition, of para- or psi-phenomena, telepathy, clairvoyance and precognition, as well as of healing. They can help us to get in touch with our roots, anchoring us in the ground of being, beyond the personal realm, beyond time. In other words, that our life experiences are there from our birth for a purpose, belonging to our karma and it is for us to bring them to consciousness and integration.

We come now to the proximal ulnar side of our palm. Luna is the goddess of the night. The root of the word luna, or moon, being the Greek *men,* which is related to *menos,* or soul, but also to spirit. Etymologically it is associated to *menoinan,* to meditate, and *memona,* to have in mind – as well as the Latin word *memoria.* Also along the same lines are mantei, prophecy; *menuo,* to reveal; *mentiri,* which means to lie, and *mania,* which means madness.[1] This light of the dark night is the inner light of imagination, creativity, dreams and symbols. This is the source of our creative intuitions and phantasies. Our dreams stem from this area of unconsciousness. In its negative attributes it is the night of unconsciousness, the flight from reality into dream-world, phantasy and hysteria, the depths of possible melancholia up to deep depression. It means to be lost in the night and in the dark; our imagination can turn into hallucinations and Luna then becomes lunacy. Hermes, as Lord of the roads, opposite

1. I am indebted to Ken Newman, "A Psychological Interpretation of the Tarot Major Arcana" (Diploma Thesis), 1975. By kind permission

Luna, can show us the intricate ways in and out of the maze. He can lead or mislead us through our "night," through our unconscious. Hermes opposing Luna can cheat us into believing that phantasies and phantoms are realities. As master of communication and language, Hermes can draw from Luna's well of creativity, imagination and language of dreams, and bring them into consciousness, whether rhetorically or in writing, or any other form – such as scientific discoveries that stem from the source of imagination and intuition. Being the prototype for the "child" energy, his connection to the night's light can point to the possibility of renewal, which the child archetype, in fact, represents. The "child" emerges from the dark womb, the inner night, where all things gestate. All our forms of creation stem from this womb. Just as in the well-known "night-journey of the soul," the most difficult phase in analysis draws its energy from this place, where the light to be found is just a reflection of the light of the sun, of consciousness. However, we can also be lost in the dark night without Ariadne's thread to lead us out of the maze. Here Hermes leads us astray. Our lunar source of inner wealth needs Apollo's art forms and Hermes' forms of communication to become manifest in all our inner and outer dealings, adding depth and imagination to our lives. Our "passive" side is, in fact, full of activity which needs to be acknowledged. It is through the activity of our inner world that we can form relationships to ourselves and to others.

Also here, in the Luna mount, it is important to have some secondary lines coming up towards the stabilizing line and towards the distal part of the palm, showing a flow from the unconscious towards other regions of our psyche. When, for instance, there are no lines on the mount and the mount is prominent, it portrays an accumulation of contents in the unconscious that have no proper channel to manifest themselves, causing inner irritation. Too many small lines may show hysterical outbursts. One or two distinct lines coming up from this mount will emphasize the urge to create and bring forth unconscious contents. When the stabilizing line stems from Luna, it shows that the person has to find his or her own special way in life, as it stems from the region of inner resources of creativity and the wealth of the imagination. We can say that the person must bring his "dream" into reality.

The upper part of Luna shows the zone that Debrunner designated as the personal unconscious material, the things that have been forgotten or repressed during the person's life, and also psychic contents that are incompatible with the conscious attitude. Its opposite pole is the zone where the thumb usually juts out or the beginning of its start away from the palm, its root. So, chirologically, this zone is crucial for ego formation. Lines here can show complementations or oppositions to the foundation of the ego. Cross lines tend to show negative experiences, upgoing lines show positive ones and downward lines show negative functioning. Here the fear lines are most prominent, although they stem already at the root of the mount. Both of these two zones encompass our basic sexual urges, "gut" feelings, phantasies, illusions, delusions and creativity. They may be associated with the "primary process."

Above Luna lies Mars, in the middle zone of the ulnar side of the palm, between Luna's and Hermes' mounts. Mars is the god of war, the warrior power of endurance, fighting force and aggression. He personifies our abilities to persevere, to hold on, to fight for and be forceful in reaching our goals: aggression both positive and negative, the latter being manifest in anger, spite, brutality and crushing power. It can also operate passively but nonetheless very forcefully and lethally as passive aggression. This is seen when the mount is flat. I have often wondered why

Mars is on the unconscious side of our palm. He seems to belong more to consciousness rather than to unconsciousness. Mars in the passive unconscious part of our palm is a "masculine" element within the "feminine" realm; just as Aphrodite is the "feminine" element within the "masculine" realm of consciousness, in the radial part of our palm. Both fulfill the yin/yang wholeness in these realms. Mars and Hermes are the active male energies respectively for our unconscious to become activated and redeemed into consciousness. Without them the unconscious remains unconscious and passive. Lines on this mount can show us our reactions to possible attack and how we counter-attack. This can also be seen at the end of the lower traverse line, called the head line.

The *head line* portrays the kind of thinking we possess, whether it is penetrating, investigating, superficial, practical or deep. It starts either connected to the end of the thenar line, close to the thumb, or independent of it. The forms of thinking are either portrayed as dependent – when the line goes some way with the thenar life line – or objective, when it is separated from the life line. When it is high up in the mount of Zeus/Hera it will convey unrealistic ambitions, contaminating the thinking function. It is not "in touch" with the life force, it is, so to speak, "high up in the air." Its ending and direction will point to the kind of thinking, the kind being determined by the finger which influences it, and the direction shows degrees of thinking. The straighter the line, the more it will tend to show practical, combative thinking, especially when it ends on Mars' mount. The more it tends towards Luna, the deeper the thinking, which may even tend towards and reach depression. Depression brings us to the depths of our being, but it can also lead us to the well of creativity residing there. This also depends on the form of the hand. For example, in a conic form which belongs to suggestible and labile personalities, this kind of line will increase the possibility of depression, whereas in a square form of hand it will show the ability to go deep and not remain on the surface of facts and figures. Here is where we see the defence mechanisms of rationalizations, intellectualizations, repressions and denials. This can be seen when the line of adaptation stops at the head line and when there are no secondary lines in the middle zone. When the head line is humped it shows concealments, when it is snake-like it shows an inquisitive mind.

The head line points to the opposites of Aphrodite/Dionysus and Mars, as it starts at one side of the palm and ends towards the other. Looking at both Mars and Aphrodite/Dionysus as opposites, we see that love, joy and the life force are connected to war; i.e., war, passion, grief and ecstasy are archetypally and chirologically connected; they are on the same continuum. This can be seen most forcibly in times of war, for example, when sex flourishes, as well as ecstasy. Love, fear, anger and courage are the ingredients of our inner wars. Love can be a continuous fight and violent aggression full of hate. In the name of love many wars are fought, also within ourselves. Aggression versus love distorts and eventually annihilates it. You cannot force love, so you fight it. Operating positively, love is sustained; it gets body, so to speak. With the help of our fighting force and perseverance we can overcome obstacles, threats to our life and love, and continue to generate and give, despite adversity. We need Mars' force and the enthusiasm and joy of Dionysus to operate in all our deeds, the loves and battles of our life. For all of these we need love as a protective, holding generative energy. Without Mars, our ego, located in the thumb opposite Mars, cannot function well. It gives the warrior power to our ego in his functions of willing, choosing and executing. Negatively, it can cause our ego to be too aggressive.

According to myth,[1] Mars, as Ares, together with Aphrodite, had two pairs of children. Eros and Harmonia as one pair, and Deimos (panic, fear) and Phobos (fright) as the other. We can surmise that the positive connection of Aphrodite to Ares/Mars can bring Eros/Harmonia into our lives. Eros, as caring and relating, is the outcome of love and perseverance: Eros is the loving force of endurance and holding on, the warrior's energy combined with love. Harmonia denotes the quality of flowing with, the "tuning in" to the spirit permeating our senses, the intimacy of "being with." At the opposite pole is the negative connection of Aphrodite to Ares/Mars. This brings panic, phobias and paranoia. Love and war as opposing energies represent striving for power and victimization, the cradle of most of our pathologies. Our pathologies may begin even before our physical birth, in the period of gestation and during the birth process.[2] Chirologically, we can see traumas happening in these stages both in the mounts of Mars and Aphrodite/Dionysus and in the formation of the lines between them. Also traumas in childhood such as sexual abuse or identity problems can be seen in the mount of Aphrodite and the thenar life line. Many lines in this area falling into the mounts of Aphrodite/Dionysus as well as Neptune/Hades show paranoid tendencies as can be seen in Picture 49.

1. Karl Kérenyi, *The Gods of the Greeks* (London: Thames and Hudson, 1974), p. 71
2. Stanislav Grof:*Beyond the Brain* (Albany: State University of New York, 1985)

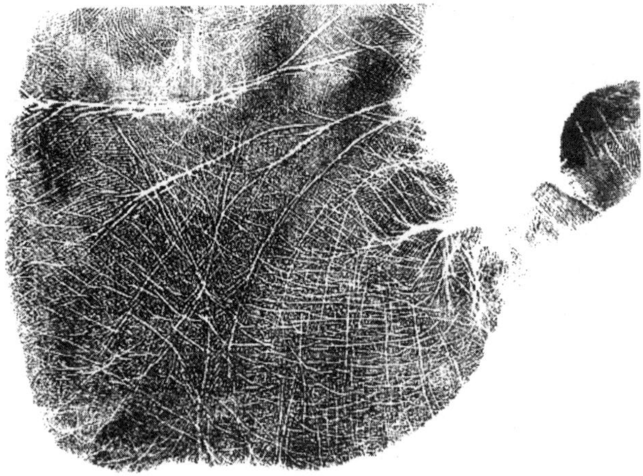

Picture 49

Mars can add force to our self-destruction; opposite the sublimation zone of the Aphrodite/Dionysus mount, it shows our ego's ability to sublimate our aggressivity by elevating it. Love, care and joy can also be elevated and utilized to service for others.

The upper traverse heart line shows the evaluating feelings. It starts under the fourth finger, Mercury/Hermes, and ends either on the mount of Zeus/Hera or between the fingers of Zeus/Hera and Saturn/Athena, the first and second fingers. It may be curved or straight, short or long, deep-set or high-set. When it is high-set it shows lightheartedness, or superficial kinds-of feelings. The lower it is set, the deeper the feelings. It may be as deep as the head line's beginning, which will sometimes point to the predominancy of feeling values over thinking.

These two lines may converge, forming almost one line. It has to be distinguished from a head line traversing the whole palm or a heart line traversing the palm, which is usually called the semian line. It cuts the palm into two sections, so to speak, emphasizing extremes, either/or tendencies of thinking or feeling, or both. Dr. Debrunner used to say that to be human is to be "curved," meaning that we humans can or should aim to be flexible and open to change and flow.[1]

When the upper traverse heart line ends in a straight line on the mount, under the first finger, I call it the Apollonian/Artemisian line, as it shows impersonal feeling values, feeling judgements and emotional demands but it also can show dedication to others and to a vocation. It emphasizes Apollo/Artemis' characteristics, both positively and negatively. Because of its beginning under the fourth finger, Mercury/Hermes (the child aspect), this line also portrays our hurt "heart" vulnerabilities, our early wounds of communication with others. Disturbances in this line in the form of islands or breaks and intersecting or subsidiary lines will show these aspects.

There may be a diagonal line that connects the Aphrodite/Dionysus mount with Hermes and is called the *developmental line*, as it conveys the possibility for integration of our basic life force and vitality with Mercurial versatility. It points to the Hermaphrodite, the union of male and female energies as the completion of life. It is love combined with communication, love as an ingredient for the ignition, the spark that starts us moving within ourselves and with the other. It points to the ultimate whole person uniting within himself love and joy on his inner and outer way, to accept the vulnerable but magnificent inner child and fill him with joy and zest for life and renewal.

1. Dr. Debrunner, oral communication to the author. Dr. Debrunner did extensive research on the differences between primates, chimpanzees and humans. The hands of the primates had straight lines.

Horizontally, this zone from the ulnar to the radial side encompasses our relations to the world, our conscious and unconscious inter/intra-relationships, which are based on our feeling values and judgments (see diagram on page 99). Lines in this area under the fourth finger, Hermes, will show possibilities to form relationships. Under the third finger, Apollo/Artemis, the lines will show diagnostic abilities, intuition and interests in the various arts. Under the second finger, Saturn/Athena, they will show responsibility and/or projections. This brings to mind their connectedness. Often when we do not take responsibility for ourselves and our actions, we tend to project them onto others.

The dynamics of all these connections are seen in the lines. Here is an example of changes in the dynamics after a period of two years of psychotherapy (Pictures 50 and 51).

Picture 50 – taken at the beginning of treatment. The whole palm is meshed with lines in all directions, showing a state of confusion and imbalance, which manifested itself in irrational anxieties and paranoid feelings (symbolized by Daimos and Phobos, the children of Mars and Aphrodite). Also, as the life line is disrupted in several places, it emphasized the lack of exact borders leading to uncertainty of self-identity This person was too open to influences from the milieu. The lines on the Mars mount show aggression. The numerous lines intersecting in the centre of the palm from Aphrodite to Apollo and Hermes show an undifferentiated need to please. The heart line, ending under the second finger and the lines under that finger, show the projections which, together with the circular line surrounding the Neptune mount, emphasize the delusional aspect of these projections. The square under the first finger, above the head line, shows the malfunctioning of the Aphrodite and Hera aspects, leading to constant conflicts in the person's daily life.

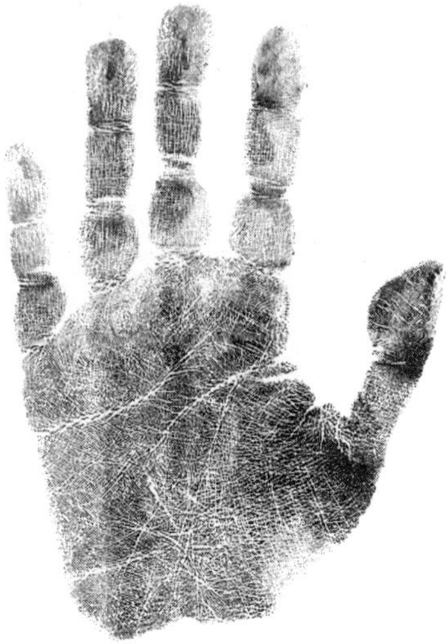

Picture 50 – taken at the beginning of treatment.

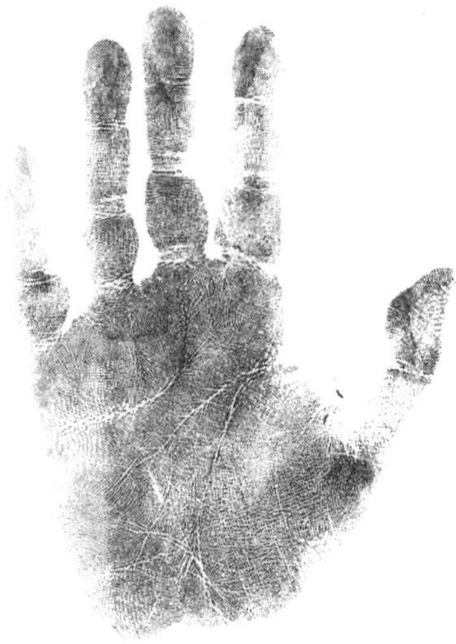

Picture 51 – taken after two years of therapy.

Picture 51 – taken after two years of therapy. Lines are more aligned, especially the thenar line, showing distinct borders in the functioning of Aphrodite/Dionysus. It also shows a process of positive alignment – more Eros and Harmonia (the children of Aphrodite and Mars/Ares) – between Mars, Neptune and Aphrodite. All the intersecting secondary lines in the ulnar part of the hand towards the proximal part in Picture 50, have almost disappeared in Picture 51. The lines remaining on Mars and connecting with Neptune, point to their positive functioning.

Picture 52, of the inner hand, shows an accumulation of disordered secondary lines on the third zone, the reality zone and the fourth zone. The head line is very straight at the beginning, showing rigid thought patterns. It forks under Saturn, the second finger, showing severe criticism. The horizontal secondary lines on the ulnar, turning towards the middle of the head line, show strong suspicion and aggressive thoughts. The heart line is full of breaks and is quite straight at the beginning until the beginning of the second, Saturn, finger, where it also forks. This shows early disruptions in the feelings and strict feeling values, complicated by ambivalency. One fork of the heart line forms a straight line which emphasizes the strict feeling values and demands, the Apollo/ Artemis functions in their hardening facets. The other fork turns under the second finger towards the first finger, showing projections, idealism, a capacity to flow with feelings towards the world, but the lines from the heart line on Zeus' mount show constant disappointments. The upper zone which is full of dispersed secondary lines shows confusion in the inter- and intra-relationships as a result of the whole conflictual thinking and feeling values, causing guilt feelings and the wilting of relationships while yearning for them. Notice the parallelism of both forks under Saturn, the second finger.

Interestingly, the upper phalange of the thumb, the domain of will power or lack of it, corresponds more or less to this zone. This implies that our will power is connected to the zone of both reality and of relationships, consciously and unconsciously, positively and negatively. We always need to relate to something or someone, in order to will and transform. Our will power for the process of transformation is necessary in order for us to be connected and committed to and in our relationships, within and without.

It is positive to have lines, but too many lines without direction show disturbances. When there are too many subsidiary lines, forming mesh-like patterns in the parts or whole of the palm, the inner disorganization is great and the drives and complexes act autonomously, as in a state of chaos. To use an example from modern physics, just as the splitting of the atom brings about an explosion of energies, so does the splitting of the self, the core, bring about explosions of autonomous complexes. In other words, the further we are from our Self, the more autonomous the drives and complexes become.

A lack of lines may show repressions, denials or externalizations up to "flattening" of the personality. All are defence mechanisms. However, a curious phenomenon occurs in extremely creative people. One can find subsidiary lines lacking in very gifted persons, such as artists whose whole life lies in their art form, be it painting, sculpture or any other artistic medium. We could say that their soul is wholly projected onto their creation: they *are* their creations.

Now we come to the expression of the lines: a curved line that has a definite direction towards another line – upward or diagonal – not too thick or too delicate, is a lively line. A line which is crude looking and thick does not portray liveliness. It may look rigid when straight, fierce when it points like a knife, cunning and resourceful when it is elastic-looking with a flow. As mentioned before, Debrunner believed from his research on primates, that to be human is to be "curved," round, flowing and with opposite poles connecting diagonally. Lines change: they are formed or extinguished, change their course and their expression. They have a life of their own and they tell their own tales.

Psychological disturbances may appear in the artistic productions of patients before the onset of psychosis.[1] So, too, in the hand one can see the process of pathology or the formation that may lead to it. As in our dreams, there is a foreshadowing of what is going to happen in our psyche. This may also herald tendencies and capabilities for the restoration and development of the personality, long before the person is conscious of it or manifests these tendencies in his behavior.

1. Silvano Arieti, *Interpretation of Schizophrenia* (New York: Basic Books, 1974), p. 352, quoting Karpof

V. Sample Chirological Consultations

We shall now illustrate practical sample procedures of some of the factors described in the over view in the preceding chapters. As each person has their own unique structure and dynamics, it must be borne in mind that the following illustrations are to show the procedure – the contents pertaining to one hand cannot be a paradigm for other hands. Nothing in the chirological test stands by itself. The same rules that operate in quantum physics[1] appear to be constellated in chirology. The meaning of any part is derived from the interconnectedness and interrelations between each part and to the whole. Each part can be seen differently depending on the question posed.

The properties of the different parts of the hand, whether they be the fingers, lines or mounts, are defined only through their interrelationships and interactions. As another parallel from quantum physics, we find in the hand also that,

> "The world appears as a complicated tissue of events in which connections of different kinds alternate, overlap, or combine, and thereby determine the texture of the whole."[2]

The procedure of a hand examination is first to take a print of the inner palm. This is done by smearing a special black ink on the palm and fingers and then pressing the hands on to a sheet of paper. When the hands are on the

1. Fritjof Capra, *The Tao of Physics,* (Shambhala Publ., 1976)
2. Fritjof Capra, *The Turning Point* (New York: Simon & Schuster, 1982), p. 81, quoting Heisenberg

sheet just before the pressing, one can see them in their *inherent* expression, i.e., the expression of the structure. Then the person is asked to lift his or her hands on the elbows, with the outer palm facing the chirologist – this portrays the form and the expression of the current psychic state, as well as the way one presents oneself to "the other." It immediately shows the relationship between the two hands, that is, the "ancestral" hand, usually the right, and the "individual," the left hand.

If we let our fingers "speak," we see dramas before our eyes, the personification of dramatic psychic states. Where "I" can observe the "me," and the "others" in me in an imaginal situation which pertains to the present one, as we will now demonstrate with the following Examples 1-6. As mentioned earlier, when the discrepancy between the "inherent" and the "present" psychic state is great, I take pictures of both states. Sometimes the person cannot hold his or her "individual" hand straight up and needs the assistance of the chirologist to straighten it, even for a few minutes in order to take the picture. I have found this procedure to be very helpful, because seeing with our own eyes the difference and the drama has a great impact on us, as the following pictures will convey. (See also Case Study in Inherent versus Current Expression.)

We have already discussed these hands from a "Hestian" point of view but we will now examine them from the different aspects of the inner drama.

1.) The present psychic state (Picture 53) already portrays, from the outside of her hand, a woman who is unsure of herself, lacks confidence in her abilities, as shown in Picture 54, in organizing and in thinking. Her negative thought patterns rule her, she seems anonymous and sacrificing, lacking will power and is full of self-accusations.

right *left*

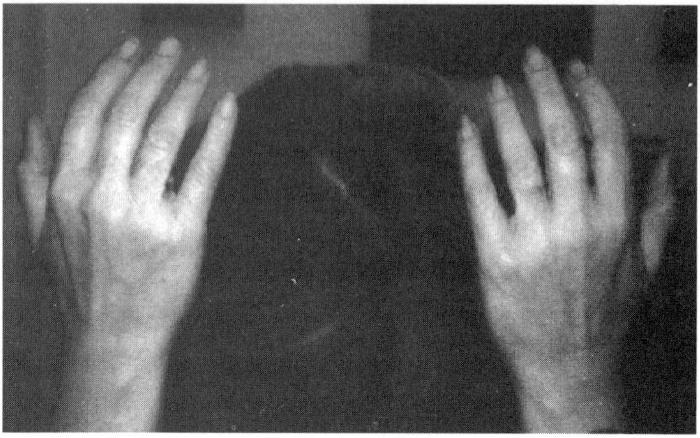

Picture 53. The thumb on both hands is bent. In the left hand, it is flatter at the top, showing lack of will power, but is of good potentiality and is seen as "emerging."

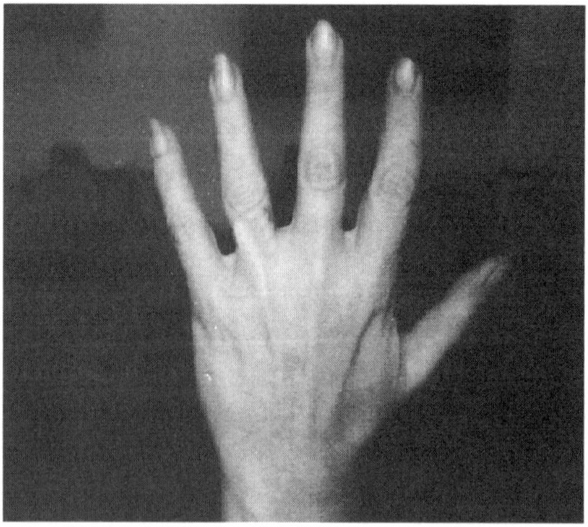

Picture 54. Inherent structure.

Picture 53 depicts the first finger in the left hand tilting towards the second finger and bent in, as Hestia (see p. 65), anonymous, sacrificing, toiling under the heavy burden of the world's demands. The middle finger shows a heavy Saturn.

In Picture 54 of the left hand we can see the inherent capabilities of Hestia at her best, although standing a bit further inward than the middle finger.

The middle finger in Picture 54 – Saturn/Athena – is ruling but as an adult, i.e., strong, sure and reasonable. The only finger which is problematic is the little finger, Mercury/Hermes, showing a frightened, almost unwanted, rejected little child (compare the expression of the fourth finger with that of the second).

Taking into consideration the similarity of both hands in Picture 53, there does not seem to be much conflict between the "parental" hand and her own hand which points to her continuing a well-known standard pattern of behavior. However, Picture 54 can direct the process of therapy into self-assurance and independence, utilizing her inherent talents.

This hand, without taking into account the inner lines and mounts, shows a need to strengthen the ego and an acceptance of the inner "hurt" child, so that she will be able to use her potentialities to the full. Here the mind is ruling the personality. By emerging as an adult person and understanding and accepting her own vulnerability (by taking care of the "child" within), she will be able to disengage from identification with the victim in all spheres of life.

2.) In the left hand in Picture 55, we can observe care for the right hand – all the hand tilts towards the right, but is held straight and at ease. All fingers are separated and independent of each other, showing independency.

right *left*

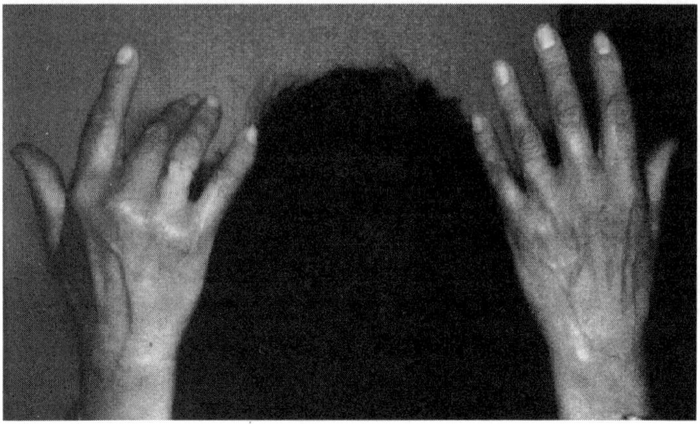

Picture 55

In the right hand we see the first finger standing up from the others – Zeus and Hera in their commanding, authoritative facets. This finger, together with the thumb, which is strong and lively, are the only upright fingers in the hand, showing their supremacy.

The middle finger is bent inward showing Saturn's heaviness and depression (the third finger – Apollo/ Artemis – is constricted and bent in). This shows that someone in the family is depressed. There is a pride in one or another family member who is authoritarian and keeps the façade of presentation towards the world. Being the "ancestral" hand, it may be all directed towards one of the parental images or one is depressed while the other is busy keeping up the "front." The fourth, Hermes, finger is quite long and is crooked at the top, which emphasizes the concealment component.

What is important here is the stand of the left hand that can help the problematics of the ancestral hand. However, it also shows a drama of these as her inner figures.

right *left*

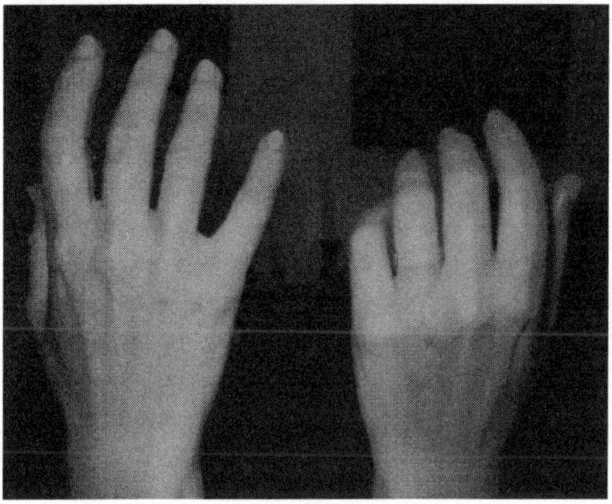

3.) Picture 56 portrays the submission of the "self" hand to the force of the "parental" hand, both on the inner and outer level. The palm in the left hand is lively and this conveys inherent forces.

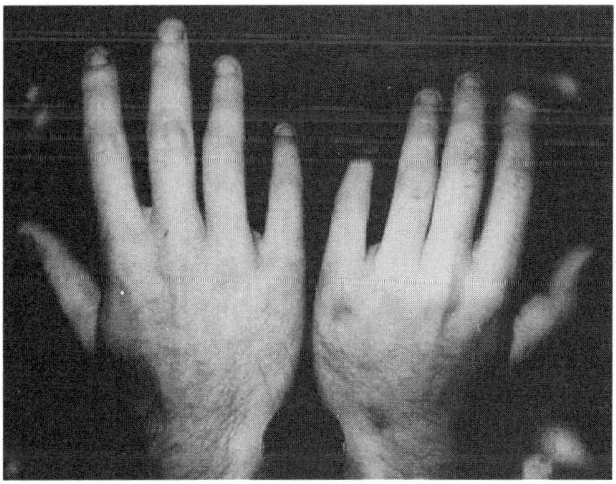

Picture 57

right *left*

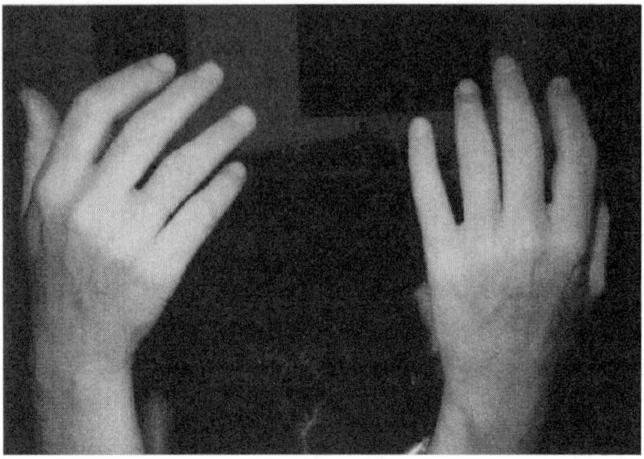

Picture 58

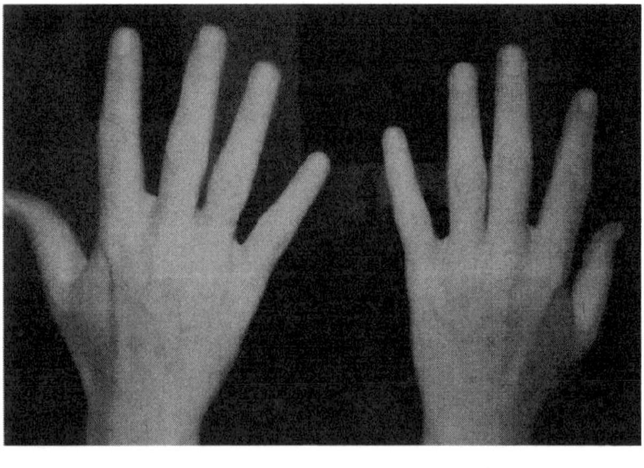

Picture 59

4.) Here (Picture 57) the left hand is crushed, belittling itself with regard to the "parental" right hand. Both hands tilt away from each other, yet the left hand ambivalently clings to the right. This shows the need to separate but the inability to do so. Notice the thumb in the left hand which is bent, indicating fear of failure.

5.) The dynamics of the hands in Pictures 58 and 59 can be interpreted as follows: The right hand of Picture 58 tilts and bends towards the left hand, as if trying to protect it. The thumb stands erect, as if watching passively. The "parental" hand is concerned. Both first fingers are bent inward, which may show a symbiosis or an overidentification between one or both of the parental figures and the subject, or vice versa, with regard to their stand in the world. However, once the left hand, the "individual," stands up, independent and active (Picture 59), the right hand, the "parental" hand can also be free and independent and gain power.

6.) Picture 60: In the present psychic state, both hands are rather limp, showing weakness. The right hand is distant. In the left hand the first finger, Zeus/Hera, is long and heavy-looking, turned inward but straight. The third finger, Apollo/Artemis, is nondescript, depicting Persephone as the obedient, compliant daughter. The fourth finger wants to get away, it looks rejecting and rejected. The thumb is weak, especially in the upper phalange.

Picture 61, the inherent capability: Once the owner of this hand can "stand up" and validate herself, all fingers change their expression. However, the "parental" hand reacts strongly and forcefully.

These dynamics portray modes of behavior that operate both on the outer and on the inner life. This is, of course, only part of the drama. The inner palm with the lines and the mounts, will give the whole dynamics, as we shall presently see.

right *left*

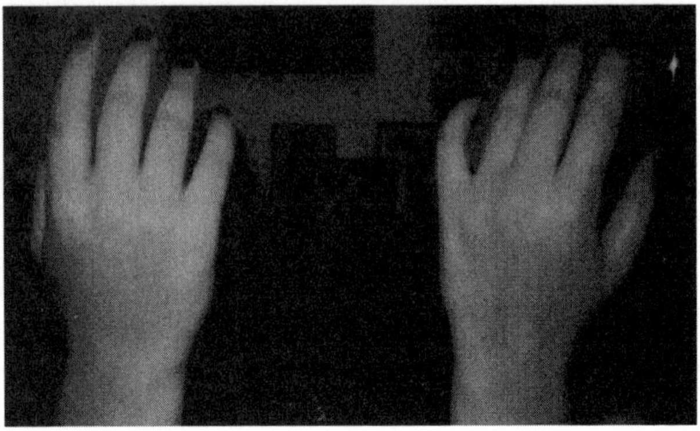

Picture 60: The present psychic state.

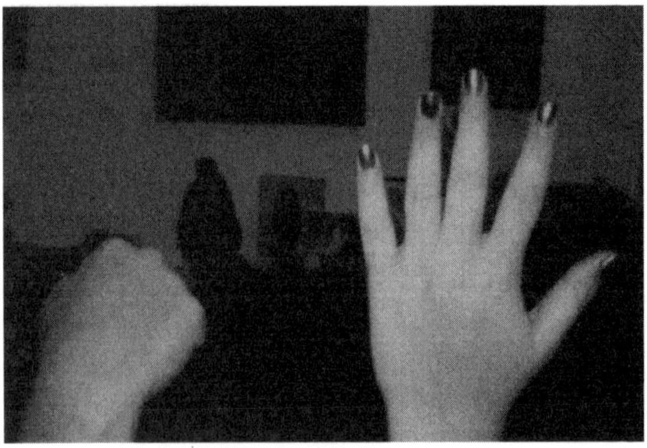

Picture 61: The inherent capability.

So far, we have interpreted the hands from their outer side. Though the information is vast, it is incomplete and can also at times be misleading without looking at the inner side of the hand. (Similar left and right outer hands may be very different when looked at internally, i.e., in the mounts and lines. Or, conversely, different outer hands can have similar inner formations of lines and mounts.) Nevertheless, these characteristics and possible dynamics can serve as guidelines for therapeutic purposes.

The next step, the "tonus," that is, the consistency of the palms, is assessed by pressing the inside and the outside of the palms in both hands. The skin texture is also evaluated. The skin is our coverage, our defence, the frontier and dividing line between us and the world. The type of skin can show its quality. When the skin is of a supple texture, it conveys an harmonious interplay between the outside world and ourselves. When the skin is thick it conveys what one calls an "elephant" skin. The person protects him or herself under a thick layer, that is, they can withstand storms and difficulties and remain sturdy and unaffected basically. When, however, the skin is delicate, thin, or even transparent, it conveys degrees of vulnerability and lack of protection.

Following this procedure, the *form* of the hands and their expressions as well as each finger's form, expression and relationship to the adjacent fingers are assessed, as well as the phalanges.

The person is also asked to let his or her hands fall, facing the table with the palms. Sometimes the person holds up his/her hands quite closed like a shield, or straight and apart. When they fall on the table one on top of the other, Spier discovered that this conveys discrepancies between what the person presents to "the other" and what is within, especially with regard to inter-relationships in the family. When they fall only on the finger-tips, forming a hole, so to speak, in the mid-palm, it conveys concealed fears. Some people find it difficult to simply let the hands fall – they put them down.

The final stage is to examine the height of the mounts in the inner palm. The order of the heights, as well as the lines on them, or stemming from them, will indicate which is paramount and active, and which is passive.

Here is a sample of a general evaluation: These are the hands of a woman in her late thirties, who came because of feelings that something was amiss in her life, although she functioned well in her day-to-day life. As the discrepancy between the "inherent" structure and the present psychic state was great, pictures were taken to show her her capabilities (Pictures 62-65, next page).

Both hands are of a conic-rectangular form, implying an impressionable personality, open, curious, receptive and flexible. The tonus of the hand is also flexible. In both hands the heart, the upper line, and head, the middle line, are curved in opposite directions. The heart line starts under the fourth finger and goes towards the radial first finger in a sweep. The head line starts under the first finger, Zeus/Hera and goes downwards to the ulnar side of the palm. In the left hand print the turn downward is even more pronounced in the lower fork at the end of the head line. It emphasizes the cyclic tendencies of the conic form. The rectangular form, however, stabilizes these tendencies and adds order and boundaries to the structure.

Both palms are lively in expression in Pictures 62 and 63.

Looking at the back of her hand and fingers, we can see a combination of both the square and the oval forms. The fingers are rectangular. The oval form indicates the inherent need for change and new experiences, yet her capabilities as expressed in the fingers are structured and adhere to rational verifications. This is a very good combination because it shows the flexibility and the eagerness of the personality for change but not at all costs.

Looking at the present psychic state as portrayed in Picture 62, we can see the "ancestral" (right) hand tilting towards the left, whereas the left, "individual" hand is straight but a little bent in and passive and also somewhat dejected. The thumb is close to the palm, almost under the first finger, showing dependency of the ego on collective rules of social behavior – Zeus' and Hera's decrees. The third finger is under the second finger – Artemis turned Persephone – the dutiful daughter's psychology. The fourth finger – Hermes – is away from the other fingers, yet bent straight, inwards. The child aspect seeks independence but Hermes' way of communication is submission yet with a streak of rebelliousness. When we compare this with the expression of the "inherent" structure in the left hand (Picture 63), we see an independent, lively personality. The thumb is lively and independent, showing good will-power and decisiveness; a person who knows what she wants and is capable of executing her decisions. Both first and second fingers are long, dominant and expressive, portraying Hera/Zeus at their best, together with an agile Saturn/Athena. The hand is purposeful and active. This, then, is her potentiality.

Having taken all the particulars of the hands, we proceed to verify and designate the characteristics as they are portrayed in the ancestral hand. We ask, as before, for the hands to be lifted on the elbows, outer hands facing the chirologist. We proceed by posing questions about the characteristics seen both in the lifted hands and in the prints, as to whom they pertain. They may pertain either to the mother, father, spouse, or even grandparents or other relatives. We may inherit capabilities of our forefathers that lie dormant in our psyche. Thus, we may reconnect to these figures, learning to utilize our inherited traits for our own development.

right *left*

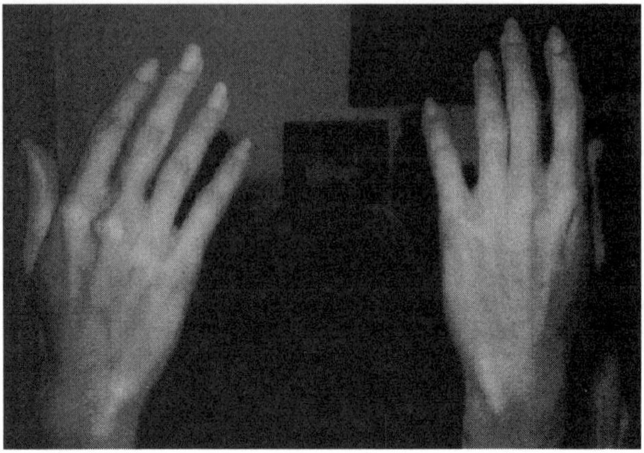

Picture 62 – present psychic state.

right *left*

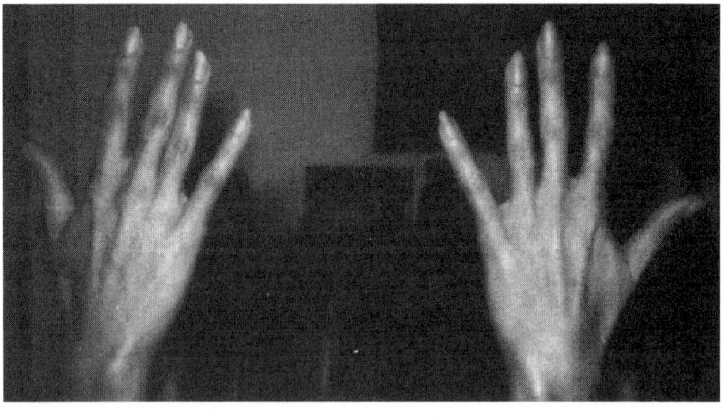

Picture 63 – inherent psychic possibility.

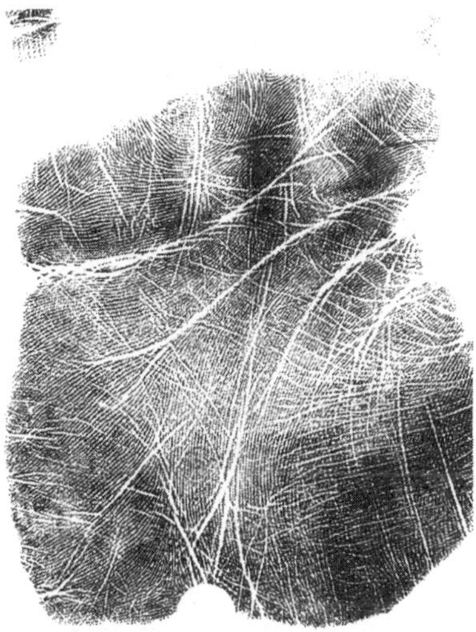

Picture 64 – left hand

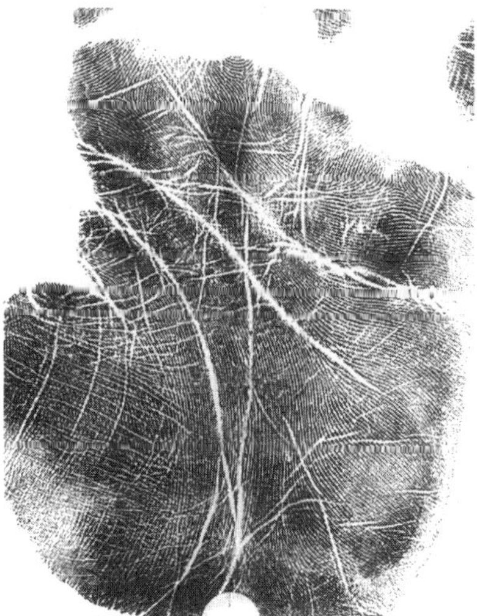

Picture 65 – right hand

The parental images portrayed two very strong personalities. The mother, according to her description, has a very strong persona, not showing outwardly what she, in fact, feels. This can be seen in the first and second fingers in the right hand, which are a bit forward, whereas the third and fourth fingers are bent in; also in the curvature of the head line (Picture 65). The mother has difficulties in showing her feelings, and can be very cold and closed off, not able to form a relationship. Notice that there are no distinct vertical lines between the fourth and the third fingers above the heart line (Picture 65). These secondary lines show an ability to form intimate relationships. In this hand there is one such line under the fourth finger (Hermes). This, together with the long fourth finger emphasizes the ability to communicate on an intellectual, social or business basis. Also notice that under the second finger on the heart line there is a horizontal line connecting with lines coming from the head line. This, together with a long second finger, a stern Saturn, indicates that her thinking dominates her personality. She has put herself under the strict discipline of her collective thinking and behavior, which is negating her own individuality, up to becoming a martyr. This can be seen in the dominance of the finger, which stands slightly more forward than all the other fingers. There is no mount under it, rather a hollow instead, emphasizing the restrictive martyr aspect of Saturn. The thumb is thick, showing a strong will-power. The adaptation, fate, line is very close to the thenar line indicating the collective approach and a need to belong. There is a diagonal line which is intersected, coming from the ulnar proximal side, the Luna mount, yet not connected to any other line except one coming down from the fate line. This shows that there is an urge coming from the Luna mount for self-expression, yet at some point it stopped and later joined in with the straight collective adaptation, the fate line. Her mother, she said, had artistic inclinations, but did nothing about them.

In Picture 62, the first finger is bent in and under the second finger and she has protruding knuckles in all her fingers, showing restriction, inhibition and a demand for orderliness. However, there is warmth and friendliness underneath. The thenar line on the whole is round, the consistency of the hand is soft and the layout of the main lines is in harmony, forming what Debrunner called the "M" form, meaning that they are well-defined. The mount of Aphrodite and the thenar line are on the whole alive and curved, showing a possibility for love, but the auxiliary lines stemming from the mount stop at the head line, showing negative thought-forms blocking the flow. Here, too, the curvature of the head line shows an amiable personality. This is a confusing "double message." She has, as we mentioned, artistic inclinations but too high aspirations. This can be seen in the expressive third finger and the too-high-up head line in the inner print of the right hand. The bulging knuckles under the first and second fingers show discord between ideals, ambitions, and reality. This, together with the high head line, starting under the first finger and its thickness, reflects her being possessed by her unrealistic opinions, and not being in tune with her body, i.e., physical strength and needs. Notice the horizontal line between the heart line and the head line. It stems also at the end of the fate line, which here stops at the heart line but continues a bit later at two points. This shows an inclination to come to sudden decisions out of an emotional outburst. Coupled with this horizontal line it emphasizes the judgemental feeling values in conjunction with her opinions, making what is called in Jungian terms, an animus possession. There is a break in the thenar line at the proximal part of the palm and the line goes towards the fate line, showing a tendency to procrastinate. This also was designated to the mother.

The father, according to her description, is also very strict, rigid and obstinate in his thinking and behavior. In Pictures 62 and 63, the second finger of the right hand is rigid-looking, the thumb strong and decisive. He is a leader, a manager who knows how to authorize and dominate. Notice the dominancy of the first finger, which is well proportioned and very expressive in Picture 63. He is also very quick in finding solutions to situations and problems, pragmatic, resourceful and spontaneous. The fourth finger, Hermes, in Picture 63 is very alive and expressive. The thumb, as mentioned previously, is lively and outgoing. The whole expression of the right hand in Picture 63 has vitality. If one compares these fingers and expression with the ones in Picture 62 they are less alive and more inward and "closed." The father is independent, warm and good-hearted, yet domineering. This can be seen in the space between the fingers in Picture 62, in the long first finger, and in the heart line in the inner print of the right hand, which has an upward curve ending at the side of the first finger. However, the other line going under and ending at the first fingers may indicate, among other things, a tendency to extremes.

These are her reactions when she was confronted with the two photos. To Picture 62 she said: "I do not like the relationship between the second and the third fingers of the left hand. Also I do not like the fourth finger being alone and inward." As to the right hand, she said: "This hand looks more spontaneous, more balanced. There is an ambivalent relationship between the right and the left hand, a relationship of attraction and repulsion. Attraction of the right towards the left and repulsion of this attraction of the left away from the right hand." To Picture 63, she said: "Here the left is freed. One step forward in development. The right hand retreats, becomes more closed." And, with an exclamation, she said: "Look! the third finger in the right hand is together and a bit under the second finger, whereas the left hand is free."

This experience was overwhelming for her. When she was told that the right hand represents her parental images working within her, she realized how much she is still dominated by these images and, in fact, lives out their problems.

Following the parental assessment we turn to the particulars of the individual person. In this sample the individual hand is on the whole very similar to the parental, showing that she is very much like her parents; a cyclic personality, spontaneous and easily provoked. This can be seen in the left inner print of the palm, the upward turn of the heart line and the thenar life line, and also in her thumb, which has a narrow "waist." However, as Picture 62 shows, she is a bit passive, disowning and renouncing her full potentialities and ability to execute them in her life. Notice the hand's expression. It is passive yet alive; the fingers are bent in, the first and fourth fingers separated, the third finger under the second finger and the thumb close to the palm and inward.

Her Artemisian traits are seen in her strict feeling values – notice the straight beginning of the heart line and the delicate auxiliary line that goes from the heart line towards the head line. It starts under the third finger, Apollo/Artemis. Her rational side dominates her personality and her feelings tend to be rationalized, suppressed or rejected. This can be seen in Picture 62 where the third finger is under the second. In Picture 63, the second finger is seen to be very long. The whole section of the heart line under the fourth finger is full of interruptions and upheavals, showing the early psychic wounds of her childhood, which can also be seen in the rectangular formation at the base of the thenar line and the milieu and fate (adaptation or stabilizing) lines. Her way of coping with them was repression (very few and faint auxiliary lines between the thenar and head lines, Picture 64), rationalizations (fate line stopping at the head line) and self-deceit, acting "as-if" (head line too high and away from the thenar line with a curve). Like her mother she, too, has unrealistic aspirations and thought forms. She tends to idealize and live in illusions and projections. The heart line in the left inner print of the palm, has an upward turn under the second finger, and the head line starts high up under the first finger. She demands of herself and others unrealistic goals, paying dearly with self-recriminations, guilt, anger and depressive moods. Her second finger is very long, showing a too severe super-ego. Notice in the print of the left inner hand, the "open square" under the second finger (two lines at one side of the finger and one line at the other side of it, with a horizontal line connecting them on the mount of the second finger). This correlates to the severe super-ego seen in the too-long second finger. It is also emphasized in the lines coming out of the heart line and falling towards the head line. The anger and the self-criticism can be seen at the fork formed in the head line, and the rather thick head line ending on the Mars mount, which is prominent in her hand. Yet, the curve upward of the head line's upper fork shows an ability to get out of difficulties, at times, by manipulation.

All this brings her to be at odds with her proper identity. Notice also the thenar line's interruptions and the fate line "taking over," so to speak, to form the continuation of the thenar line at this juncture. However, the very beginning of the thenar line is well-formed, the mount is prominent and this shows her inherent good inner ground and zest for life, Aphrodite's realm of love and generosity. Dionysus' joy is missing as the mount at the base is lacking in lines, just as in the right hand print, she is cut off from her instincts.

Looking at Picture 63, which shows her inherent capacity, one can see vigor, independence, free ability to decide and to choose. The thumb is independent of the palm, decisive and well-proportioned. The fingers stand firm with space between them, yet the first and the fourth stand alone, the second and third close to each other. This means that her feeling and thinking are connected, yet with a possibility for harmony between them. Picture 63 reveals her Zeus/Hera attributes, an ability for leadership, organization and expansion. The first and second fingers being longest, emphasize the dominance of conscious activity, recognition and extraversion. Her second, Saturn/Athena finger is slender, expressive and very long, showing her agile thinking function, Athena's presence as a friend and advisor, as well as a "puella" facet. The third finger is expressive although it is short in comparison to the first finger. She has a very strong artistic side which, however, has not yet found its full expression in her life. Notice the closure in the print under the third and fourth fingers. This also indicates difficulties in forming relationships; she feels lonely and inwardly withdrawn, her fourth finger separate, standing alone and inward. Hermes, the spark of life, that new energy which starts things going, is still inhibited. She is conflictually attached to her home and parents, needing them yet resisting them. Notice the fate line attached to the thenar life line, with many breaks and interruptions.

Yet there are diagonal lines, one stemming from Neptune towards Hermes. It is not a flowing line but it seems to be striving forward, showing an inner urge to find ways to get out of the situation and become conscious. The other diagonal lines are higher up stemming from the thenar and fate lines towards Hermes, nearer to Apollo. This is the mercurial developmental line, conveying the possibility for integration of her basic life force and vitality with Mercurial versatility. It points to her possibility to become a "whole" person, accepting with love her vulnerable inner child and filling it with joy and zest for life and renewal.

What transpires out of these photos and prints so far, is the unconscious identification of the woman with her negative mother image. The negative aspects of both parental images with regard to the dominancy of the thinking function, rules over the whole of her personality. What she lacks are the positive aspects of the father image in herself, i.e., her own "masculine" capabilities to direct her life and to free her ability to choose and carry out her inherent capacities. She needs to separate herself from this parental bonding in order to become an individual in her own right.

Second Example

This is a hand of a woman in her mid-thirties. She is right-handed. The form of the hand tends to be between conic and rectangular and of average size. When dividing her hand into palm and fingers, we can see a palm which combines within it both the square and the conic forms. The fingers are also a combination of conic, at the lower part, and rectangular, towards the nails (Picture 67). This indicates general characteristics of an impressionable personality, with a tendency to extremes, yet also an inherent ability for boundaries and form.

While the prints of the hands were taken, the inherent expression of the outer left hand presented itself, as seen in Picture 67. The expression of the structure of the hand is between weak and lively but the thumb is lively and rather strong, tending outwards. The palm has life in it but "feels" emerging into life. (Compare the expression of the palm in Picture 66.)

right *left*

Picture 66: Present psychic state.

Picture 67: Inherent structure of left hand.

However, when the woman was asked to lift her hands on her elbows, with the outer hand toward the chirologist, her left hand looked quite different from the expression of the structure of the hand, as seen in Picture 67. Picture 66 shows her present psychic state. This is the "normal" or usual way this woman holds up her hands in this period of her life. It shows weakness, sadness, tending to depression, lack of belief in herself, subdued. The expression of the whole hand and how it is held, shows diminution of energy. The fingers are tending towards the body and closed. The fourth finger is separated and bent-in even more. The thumb is very close to the palm, yet retaining its vigor. The overall expression is of compliance.

Let us now consider the right hand in both Pictures. In Picture 66 the hand tends towards the left hand, also bent in. It looks stronger than the left hand, as if subduing it. In Picture 67 the expression is different. The hand is more upright; the fingers look rigid, tending towards the body but straight and tending away, towards the radial side of the hand. The whole hand is away from the left hand, as if in defiance. Two knuckles, under the first and second fingers, are protruding while first finger is heavy and strong.

Going a step further, let us use the imaginary description of the relationships between the right and the left hand, i.e., between the parental images and the person. What does this chirological description convey to us about this woman's present psychic state? (Picture 66) We can imagine the following self-description: "I feel low, resigned, sad and even depressed under the heavy load of the demanding yet protecting parental images. They put pressure on me in their depression and constrict me and they are themselves constricted. I dare not 'lift' myself up, yet I resent this situation. If I do try to rise up (Picture 67) they will distance themselves from me, become very rigid and judgmental and I shall be hurt." (Third finger in the left hand is under the second finger, hesitant and bends in a little. Fourth finger bent inwards, but rather straight.)

Let us now examine how the personality of this woman is dynamically expressed in the print of the palm. The right palm (Picture 68) has less distinct auxiliary lines. The lower traverse line (the head line) is low in the hand, as if "sitting" on the thenar line, the life line, meaning that thinking is suppressing the life force. This line, the head line, tends down towards the Mars and Luna mounts, emphasizing the depressive tendency that we saw in the outer hand. The upper traverse line (the heart line) is wide and with many breaks in the flow of it. It is rather straight and only under the second finger does it tend upwards, ending with a fork. One leg of this fork continues straight, ending on the mount under the first finger, whereas the second leg of the fork tends upwards towards the side of the second finger. The line and the first fork emphasize the demanding and judgmental attitude – Artemisian qualities – whereas the line with the second fork shows the warm and giving side of the parental images. Above this line we can see a semi-circular intersected line that indicates, in this specific case, utmost sensitivity. Under the second finger we can also detect a closure with a line coming up or down from the side of the third finger, indicating that everything comes in difficulties and heaviness; difficult life experiences. In the outer hand there are protruding knuckles under the first and second fingers, emphasizing this tendency. They show conflicts between one's wishes, ideas and reality.

The parents of this woman had a very difficult life. Both of them are survivors of the Holocaust, having lost their own parents early in life. Their sole comfort and meaning in life is their daughter, who has to comply to their demands, aspirations and needs. She is their *raison d'être*, so to speak.

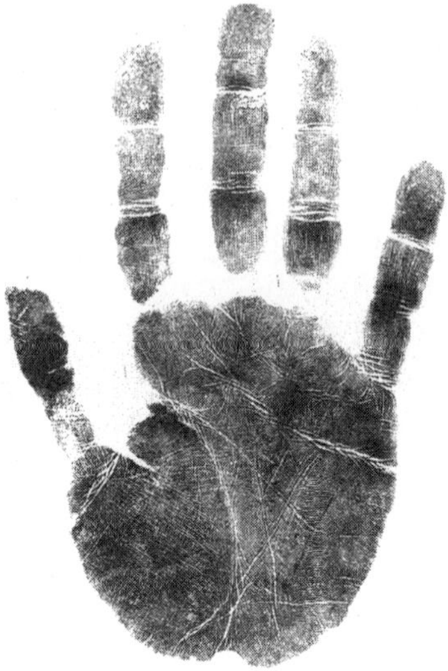

Picture 68 – Right Hand.

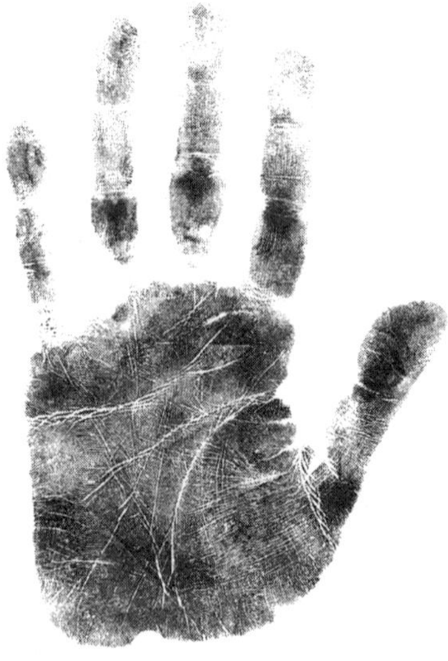

Picture 69 – Left Hand.

Looking at the left palm (Picture 69), the lower traverse line (head line) has a fork just under the side of the third finger. One leg of this fork tends downwards towards the Luna elevation with a bit of a bend at the end. There is another line at the end, parallel to the head line. The fork indicates her negative self-criticism, bringing her to depression and outward resignation. However, the continuation of this line shows her resentment, yet also indicating her intelligence and the possibility of constructive criticism – the parallel line. The upper traverse line (the heart line) has also a fork but in comparison with this line in the right hand, we can see the different essence of the expressions. In the left, the fork that continues towards the mount under the first finger has not that sharp straight line of the right hand. It has an upward trend, softer. If we use our imaginary language, it has an appealing gesture, not a demanding one. She is searching for love and relationships, for giving and being given.

The line of adaptation runs from the base of the ulnar proximal side (the luna mount) towards the leg of the fork that tends down. Another adaptation line starts also from the middle proximal side of the hand, becoming stronger at the intersection with the developmental line, that is the diagonal line going from the thenar mount towards the fourth finger. So this woman has two adaptation lines, showing the conflict between her connection to the parental images and their way, as opposed to her own individual needs of development. As it shows itself in Picture 69, this individual way is not a continuous straight line but is comprised of small lines one after the other, and it stops short of the leg of the fork coming down from the head line. At the time of the print, she was still under the yoke of the burden, not able, as yet, to utilize her need for developing her own way in her life. The mount of Luna at the ulnar side shows disorganized lines, also above at the second section of the ulnar side there are horizontal lines – this all emphasizes her unconscious strivings for self-expression, but also some paranoid anxieties and feelings of being attacked. She experiences them as disturbing inner unknown urges that cause her sleeplessness and irritability.

VI. Changes in the Hands after Psychological Work

Hands, as we have seen, are dynamic. They change with or without therapy. However, experience has taught me that there is a remarkable distinction between changes due to perpetual life experiences and changes occurring out of an inner work involving a transformational process within the personality.

The expression of the outer palm and fingers can at times, besides the present and the inherent psychic states, portray degrees of consciousness. The individual hand may look more "differentiated" than the ancestral hand. And example of this state can be seen in Picture 55 (page 124). By using the word "differentiated" I mean an expression of liveliness, somehow mature, more defined. An example of this is the feeling we have at times when we meet someone whom we sense is working on his problems and has an "aura" of being centered, or conscious. In the hand of such a person we find a physical expression of energy.

Changes in the hand-prints are easier to see and follow because the changes are in the formation of the lines or even in their disappearance. One can see in the hands of analysands where certain problems have been worked through; whereas in the hands of those not in analysis, one sees that basic problems usually remain untouched even though changes in those psychic states, for better or worse, are apparent. Also mention must be made of those cases in psychotherapy where no changes occur, either in the analysis or in the hand.

The following examples[1] show distinct changes in the hand prints due to analytical work over some years. The data of the analytical assessment and treatment were provided by Dr. Gustav Dreifuss (Haifa). A chirological test preceded the beginning of each analysis and a second chirological test was taken after a period of analysis. Changes indicated in the analysis were confirmed by the changes in the lines of the hands of the analysands.

I: Patient L. is a woman in her sixties. She is now pensioned after a successful career. She is gifted, intelligent and artistic. She suffered from the fact that she had never married and has had no children, but she was satisfied in having had a creative life and many friendships. Because of difficulties in the relationship with her man friend, she was depressed and came for a psychotherapeutic consultation. This first interview circumambulated the problem of her continuous disappointments in relationships. Her disappointment in the partner made her irritable, demanding and destructive. Some further talks on the subject were suggested, but since her immediate concrete problem at that time had solved itself, she came back for a second session only after 9 months. Now, she felt, it might be useful to find out more about her difficulties, especially in relationships, as again she experienced unrest and dependency which irritated her. The analyst felt that now analysis was really indicated, especially in view of a first dream which she had dreamt approximately a month before she came for the second time. "I had long open hair like little girls wear it today. A man (my father or my friend) combs my hair with a fine comb and finds lice in my hair."

1. These examples have been printed in my article "Psyche & Soma in Chirology: Personality Changes in analysis as reflected in the Hand," in *Spring 1974* (New York: Spring Publications).

This dream seemed to be an indication for analysis: Her animus was active in cleaning her hair, her mental products from dirt, from the lice. But, because of her age and her physical weakness there were doubts whether analysis could be risked. She was therefore sent for a chirological test, with the specific question whether the analyst's impression that the patient could undertake analysis could be confirmed.

The chirological test before beginning analysis:

A refined woman, sensitive and intuitive, and also practical and somewhat earthy. A lively hand of a conic-rectangular wide form. Middle and lower phalanges of the fingers longest.

Despite this being a good combination, it is still a source of stress and inner disharmony. (Knuckles between the base of the fingers and palm). A person of extremes: a familial and collective need to be accepted by society and yet bohemian trend making independence just as important. (The stabilizing fate line close to the thenar line. First finger long and lively; an indistinct line from the Luna mount coming diagonally to the stabilizing line.) She has strong religious (a line looking like a curved belt beginning under the Zeus/Saturn mounts going towards the thenar line), philosophical (lines at both ends under middle finger, Saturn) and parapsychological inclinations (an elevated Neptune mount and diverse lines curving from this mount towards Mars), which clash with rigid aggressive and unrealistic opinions and attitudes. (Straight head line, beginning high in the Zeus mount.) She is receptive, easily impressed, alert and quickly stimulated (conic form, expressive fourth finger. Slender lower phalange in the thumb. Lines from the Aphrodite/Dionysus mount towards Hermes). At the same time she has deep fears, and at times her intuitions,

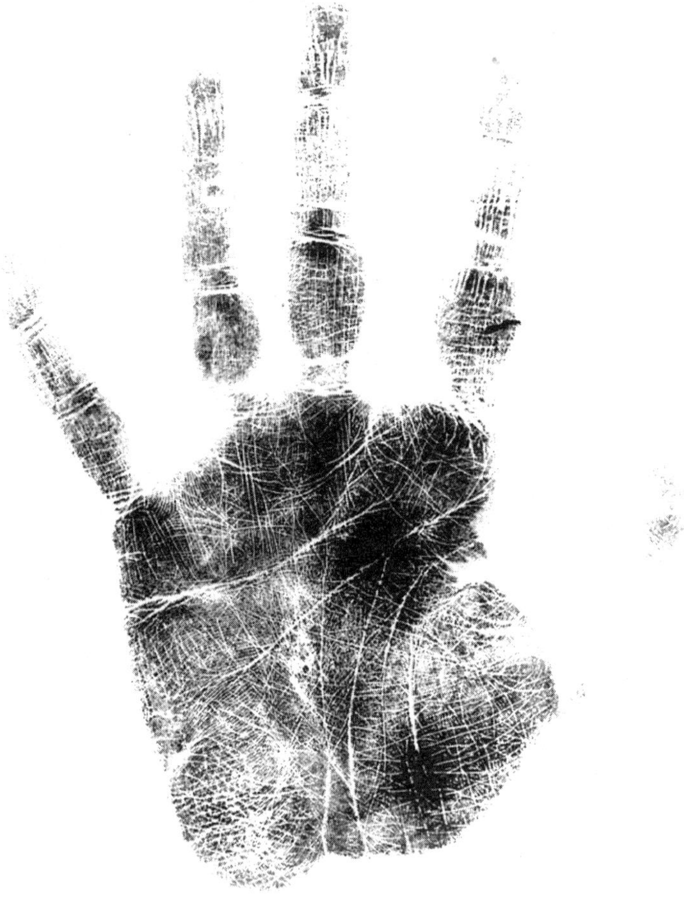

Picture 70: Left hand.

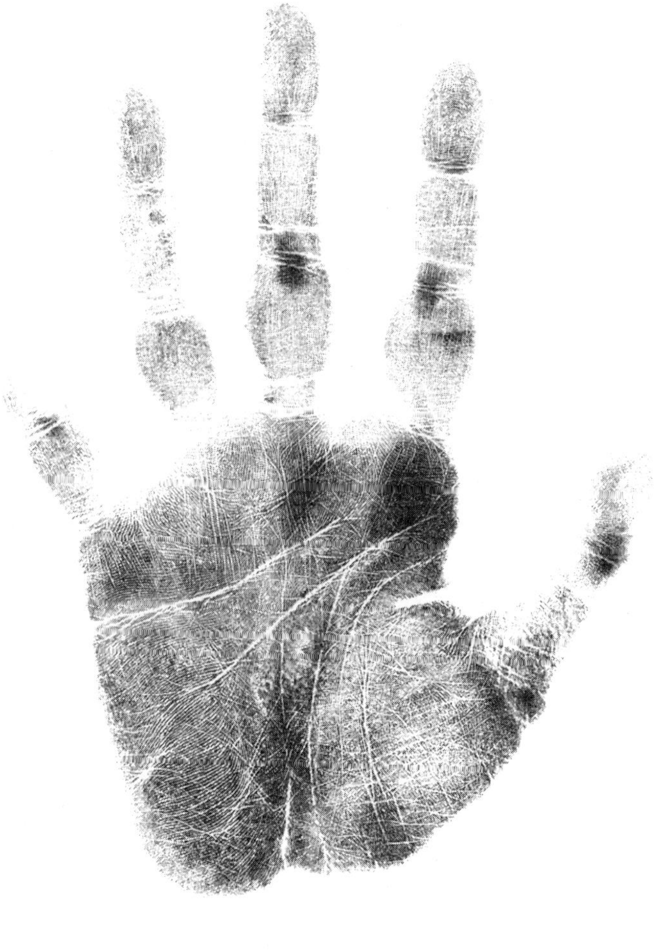

Picture 71: Left hand.

sensations, and emotions are so intense that she fears losing herself in them. (Exaggerated mesh-like lines in the Luna mount, Thenar, Aphrodite/Dionysus mount, lines coming from Mars mount towards them.)

She hesitates before deciding, and will not be able to get over things easily. (Thenar line joining head line not at the beginning of the head line but somewhere a third along the line, under the space between first and second fingers.) However, she can also be very spontaneous. (There is another thenar line which is not completely circling the mount, forming a distance between the thenar line and the head line.) It seems that she lives on two levels which causes inner stress and fears. (Two thenar, vitality lines.) Owing to rationalizations, (i.e., opinions – straight head line) she neglects the call from within. (The indistinct diagonal line from the Luna mount towards the stabilizing line, the indistinct Mercurial, developmental line, joining Aphrodite and Hermes – what I call the hermaphroditic line.) Her vitality is uneven, periods of liveliness vary with periods of laxity. (Two thenar lines.)

She is intelligent and has a scientific mind, tolerance of thought and breadth of thinking. (Long head line ending under fourth finger; lines between third (Apollo) and fourth (Hermes) fingers, especially lines under the third; a good, well-spaced area between head and heart lines.) She is ambivalent (fork at the end of heart line; two endings to heart line – a sweep under Saturn towards the beginning of this finger), very demanding and dependent, in search of a loving father. (Straight heart line when following the lower "leg" of the line, notice the many lines under Zeus' finger, i.e., on Zeus' mount joining the end of the heart line and the secondary line curving towards the head line.) Her need for love and attention bring her to states of jealousy and frustration. (Confusion of lines under Zeus/Hera finger on their mount, long and domineering Hera, first finger.) Time and again she has disappointments, owing to unrealistic expectations and demands, which depress her and bring her to distrust her feelings. (The abrupt "leg" of the heart line going upwards towards Saturn finger – emphasizing the puella aspect.) She feels very lonely, although she is capable of forming good relations with other people. (Fourth finger Hermes away from the rest of the fingers, its expression is sad, lines under Hermes' finger, on its mount.) Her father image disturbs her personal relationships. (Low set fourth, Hermes, finger in the palm.) Her aggressions and frustrations, out of a deep sense of inner dissatisfaction and feminine revolt, cause guilt and self-torture. (Meshed lines on a developed Mars mount (i.e., not flat); the disarrayed lines in the palm on the whole; Artemis third finger, lively expression; lines between Saturn/Athena and Apollo/Artemis fingers. Heavy-looking Saturn finger.)

Nevertheless, she always falls on her feet, thanks to her practicality and earthiness. She is artistically gifted (a lively expressive third, Apollo/Artemis, finger) and gives much feeling to her work. (Heart lines going on to Zeus' mount.) She has many interests which disperse her. (Too many lines on Apollo's mount). She has difficulty in perseverance and systematic work, although she is capable of doing it. (An indistinct triangle in the middle of the palm formed usually by the head line, thenar line or adaptation-stabilizing line and the developmental line. This shows an ability to persevere and do systematic work.)

As the aim of this example and the following one is to show the differences in the individual hands after a period of analysis, I shall only mention the parental images without presenting their pictures.

The parental image: The parents seem to be very different personalities and she has ambivalent feelings towards them. One parent was very dogmatic, religiously rigid, decisive, closed, ascetic, pedantic, strong yet quite sensitive, had an ability to express himself in talk. When asked which parent, she confirmed that this described her father.

Her mother, then appeared in the hand as hypersensitive (which affected her thinking), spontaneous, charming, many interests, intuitive, and musical, a cyclic personality tending at a later age to depression. There is in the patient a fear of resembling her mother. The patient suffered from the opposites of her parental images, causing an inner split between the spiritual (father) world and the practical (mother) world, losing herself in both of them alternatively.

Conclusion: an hysterical personality with many inner opposites and fears. Conversion reactions to body image and bodily health. (The meshed lines on the Luna mount, too many dispersed lines, especially at the lower proximal mounts, Aphrodite and Dionysus, and the mount of Mars, as well as in the whole palm.) Analysis is recommended.

Second chirological test:

In the second chirological test, after some years of analysis and done at the same time as but independently of, the analyst's report, the following changes were marked: Less hysterical and chaotic state, less agitation and nervousness. There is more centeredness. (Luna mount not meshed with lines. More defined and clear demarcation of thenar and stabilizing-adaptation lines). Line of fear on Aphrodite's mount. The fears are still there but less menacing. Fewer ambivalent feelings. (The upward "leg" of the heart line has almost disappeared.) Her anxieties regarding health and body image are now more focused on herself and less projected on others in her relationships. (As above.) There is more responsibility with fewer guilt feelings. (Well formed perpendicular lines under Saturn finger.) Her interests are more centralized, less dispersed. (Well arranged lines under Apollo's finger.) There is, in general, expression of more contentment, more ability to work and produce, to bring out material from the imaginative regions of the psyche which builds the personality. There is less compulsion, more unfolding, i.e., inner discipline. (Well defined lines with specific directions, upwards and diagonal.) She is less sensitive to the opinions of others. The ambition to succeed and attain her goals is there, but not in a neurotic way. (Lines on Zeus/Hera's mount defined, with less interruptions of other, secondary lines.) The unconscious is less chaotic; it is rich and active in an expressive and artistic way. More spirituality. (The basic lower mounts, especially Luna has some lines; a more distinct diagonal line coming upwards from Luna towards stabilizing-adaptation line; Aphrodite/Dionysus mount is more calm and well-defined, as well as the connection to Mars.) She is less in conflict between the two worlds she is living in. Today she tends more to become sad than aggressive and sharp-tongued. (There is a change in the ending of the head line, it looks smoother, i.e., more delicate, a quieter Mars.) She is less dependent on a male-partner. There is more personal expression and inner independence. (All fingers are similarly separated. A livelier fourth Hermes finger with well defined lines on its mount.) The analyst's report concurred with these findings.

II. (This example will not be discussed extensively, but mainly with emphasis on the concurrent change in personality and in the hands in order to elucidate further my point – see pages 156 and 157.) Patient A. is a woman of twenty-five. According to the analyst she suffered from depressive states, lack of contact, feeling alienation, isolation, and uncertainty with regard to her femininity. She

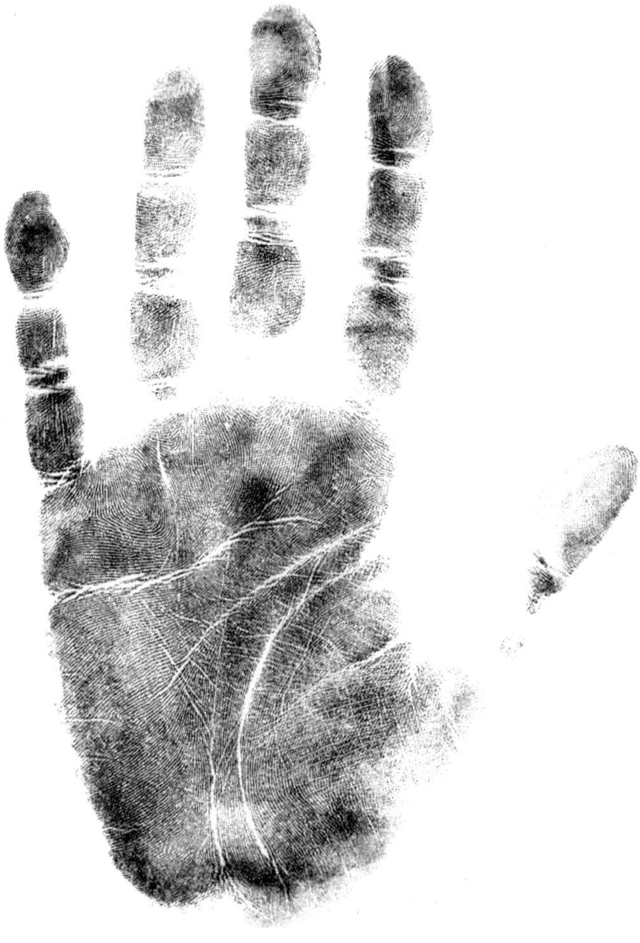

Picture 72 – At the beginning of analysis.

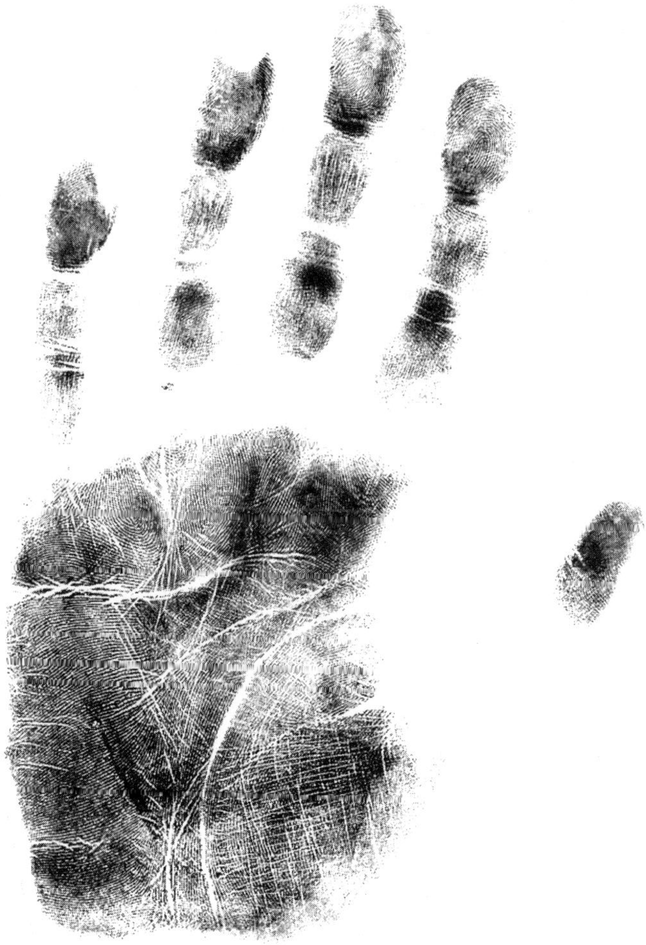

Picture 73 – Second test after four and a half years.

had negative feelings towards her parents and toward parental figures.

The chirological test confirmed his findings. She thoroughly repressed her authentic personality and denied her sensitivity. She was blocked in her feelings, thinking and relationships. The hand showed very few lines, although this type of hand usually tends to have more lines. (This is a conic-oval form of a hand.)

After four and a half years of analysis a remarkable change of feminine identity took place, showing itself in improved relationships to parents and especially to men. She married one and a half years after the second chirological test was taken and the analysis was terminated. She also satisfactorily entered into a new profession. Analytically the accent was upon developing into the world, as compared with patient L. where the accent was on inner life and creativity.

The second chirological test, which was taken after four and a half years, confirmed the changes. The whole palm is more expressive, there are more marked lines especially the line of development and relationships, which are the diagonal lines from the middle of the palm to under the fourth finger. Also there are more marked lines in the middle zone of the hand, lines of experience, which in her case show more ability to experience inner and outer happenings without closing herself off from them. However, the entire zone of the unconscious (the ulnar part of the palm) is still without enough lines in connection with other lines. This points to the fact that she has worked more on the personal unconscious and problems of reality and relationships, but not yet enough on the deeper layers of her personality.

Case Discussion from the Chirological Viewpoint – a Recapitulation

Both women have more or less the same form of hand, a conic one with rather long fingers and delicate narrow looking palm. In patient L. the palm is wider than in patient A. The conic hand, as mentioned before is the receptive and impressionable hand. Usually this hand form has many lines and is expressive.

In patient L. the hand is much too lined, even meshed-like, and through analysis some lines were extinguished and others became more ordered. The lower ulnar zone of the hand, which portrays the unconscious, was in the first test meshed with lines. This showed the chaotic state in which she then was, where the contents of the unconscious threatened to overflood her. In the second test the lines were no longer meshed. There were many more ordered lines, showing a flow from the unconscious to the conscious zone which is enriching and productive for the personality. The conflicts between the two modes of living showed themselves in the first test in various parts of the hand. However, only two of them will be mentioned here. There were multiple vertical lines under the fingers in the first test, but these were hardly visible because of many intersecting lines, especially under the first finger. In the second test the vertical lines were accentuated and less disturbed, emphasizing spiritual interests and a lessened sensitivity to her status in the world. Her ability to form and further relationships without demanding too much showed in the second test in the upper ulnar zone with fewer intersecting lines. It also showed in the same test in the first traverse line (heart line), emphasizing more focused feeling with fewer demanding projections. This line in the first test had an upward sharp turn toward the end of the second finger. In the second test the accentuation was more on the continuation of this line towards the first finger, losing its sharp upturn. The stabilizing zone, the middle part of the palm in the first test was filled with fan-like lines. In the second test this same zone had fewer lines and looked quieter; i.e., the stabilizing factor was at work with fewer conflicts.

In patient A. the situation was the reverse. Whereas this type of hand, as mentioned earlier, usually has more lines to begin with, at the beginning of analysis there were far too few lines. The two women, although belonging to the same general type of personality (receptive, impressionable, with artistic inclinations and tending to extremes), use different defense mechanisms. We cannot here go into this interesting problem of the etiology of the dynamics of the personality, as it is a subject in itself; however, in this case it may be that the wider palm in patient L. contributes to this difference in defenses, as well as the conic-oval combination of patient A, the egg form that had not 'hatched.' Whereas the first uses conversion, acting out and in, and rationalization, the second uses denial, repression, closing off and has paranoid tendencies. This shows itself in the hand in the first test of patient A. There we see a general absence of sub-lines especially in the upper zone of the palm, the distal part, under the fingers, mainly under the fourth finger. Through analysis the hand became more expressive and lively and more lines emerged, especially under the fourth finger, the zone of relationships, and under the third finger showing more interests and openness to intuition. Also here the stabilizing zone in the second test is more accentuated.

Another point of importance is that patient L. is an artistically gifted person, having at her disposal tools for inner expression; whereas, patient A. is less fortunate in this respect, although she has an artistic understanding. The age difference is in this case, not a decisive factor, but their difference in coping with their life problems is basic.

Epilogue

In the last chapter we have seen the value of chirological tests in conjunction with therapeutic analysis, both as a diagnostic tool and as an aid for evaluating process and change.

Throughout the book I have pursued the different archetypal images in their locations in the palm and in the fingers. Their specific locations confirm physically, so to speak, known psychological truths. It is interesting that long before psychological theories formed themselves, they were, already from antiquity, laid out in our hands as a map of "psychic prints." These locations are constant and are found in everybody's palm, but their manifestations are personal and unique. Like the genetic code that holds within itself the whole development of the organism, so the hand has within itself the riddle, which is our specific myth, and the possible awareness to its mystery in our lives.

As we have seen, nothing in the hand stands by itself. It is like a field of energy, everything is vibrating with meaning but the meaning is derived through the interaction of the parts between themselves and to the whole. The signs are never to be taken as "facts" but rather as "sign posts," as probabilities.

Insights emerge, as I have shown, of connections between the images that may throw light on a deeper understanding of the inner interrelationships of the different parts of our personality and for their possible transformation. What is realized is that the opposites as portrayed in the hand are also the complementary factors necessary for our wholeness. The well-known phrase that "everything is within" materializes as "body" when finding it in our own physical hand.

Over the years, looking back, the themes of our mythic life are revealed to form a story. It seems to me that the language of the hand and its wisdom can point towards a more conscious way of living. Our individuation lies in our becoming aware of its process and in trying to understand its meaning for our life.

Bibliography

A Course in Miracles (Tiburon, Calif.: Foundation for Inner Peace, 1975, 1985)

Arieti, Silvano: *Creativity, The Magic Synthesis.* (New York: Harper Colophon Books, 1976)

Bakal ed. *The Book of the Wisdom of the Hand.* Taken from the Zohar (Jerusalem)

Debrunner, Hugo: "Psychosomatische Diagnose und Therapie," *Schweizerische Zeitschrift für Psychologie und ihre Anwendung,* Vol. XVII (Bern & Stuttgart: Verlag Hans Huber, 1958)

— "Altersbedingte Handlinienänderungen beim männlichen Geschlecht," *Der Psychologe,* Separatdruck aus Heft 7/8 Bd. IV (Schwarzenburg: GBS Verlag, 1952)

Cameron,N.: *Personality, Development and Psychotherapy,* (Boston: Houghton-Mifflin, 1963)

Capra, Fritjof: *The Tao of Physics,* (Shambhala, 1976)

— *The Turning Point* (New York: Simon & Schuster, 1982)

Carus, C.G.: *Psyche* (Part I, On the Development of the Soul), (Zurich & New York: Spring Publications, 1971)

Downing, Christine: *The Goddess, Mythological Images of the Feminine.* (New York: Crossroads, 1981)

Demetrakopoulos, S.A.: "Hestia, Goddess of the Hearth," in *Spring 1979* (Dallas: Spring Publications, 1979)

Franz, Marie-Louise von: *An Introduction to the Interpretation of Fairy Tales* (New York: Spring Publications, 1970)

— *Number and Time* (London, Rider & Co., 1974)

Friedrich, Paul: *The Meaning of Aphrodite* (Chicago: University of Chicago Press, 1978)

Getting, F.: *The Book of the Hand,* (London: Hamlyn, 1965)

Greene, Liz: *Relating* (London: Coventure, 1979)

Grof, Stanislav: *Beyond the Brain* (Albany: State University of New York, 1985)

Haft-Pomrock, Yael & Ginath, Yigal: Differences between Schizophrenics and Normal Controls using Chirological (hand) Testing. *Israel Journal of Psychiatry & Related Sciences,* Vol.19, No .1, 1982

Haft-Pomrock, Yael: "Number and Myth: The Archetype in our hands," *Quadrant,* 1981 Vol. 14, No. 2

— "Chirology as a Self-Creating mirror," *Confinia Psychiatria,* 21, (1978)

— *Psyche & Soma in Chirology: Personality Changes in analysis as reflected in the Hand* (New York: Spring Publications, 1974)

Hillman, James: *On Senex Consciousness* (New York: Spring Publications, 1970)

— *The Negative Senex and a Renaissance Solution* (New York: Spring Publications, 1975)

— *Re-Visioning Psychology* (New York: Harper & Row, 1975)

— "On the Necessity of Abnormal Psychology: Ananke and Athene," in *Facing the Gods* (Texas: Spring Publications, 1980)

— "The Great Mother, her Son, her Hero and the Puer," in *Fathers and Mothers,* Ed. Patricia Berry (Dallas: Spring Publications, 1990)

Hutchinson, Beryl B.: *Your Life in your Hands* (London: Neville Spearman, 1967)

Jung, C.G.: "Structure and Dynamics of the Psyche," CW 8 (Princeton: Princeton University Press, and London: Routledge & Keagan Paul, 1960)

— "Symbols of Transformation," CW 5 (Princeton: Princeton University Press, and London: Routledge & Keagan Paul, 1956)

Kérenyi, Karl: *The Gods of the Greeks* (London: Thames & Hudson, 1971)

— *Hermes Guide of Souls* (Zurich: Spring Publications, 1976)

— *Athena: Virgin and Mother* (Zurich: Spring Publications, 1978)

— *Apollo* (Zurich: Spring Publications, 1983)

— *Zeus and Hera* (Princeton University Press, 1975)

Laing, Ronald: *The Self & Others: Further Studies in Sanity and Madness* (London: Tavistock Publications, 1961)

López-Pedraza, Rafael: *Hermes and his Children,* (Einsiedeln: Daimon Verlag, 1989)

Mangold, Ursula von: *Zeichen des Schicksals im Bild der Hand, Anlagen und Möglichkeiten* (Olten/Freiburg im Breisgau: Walter-Verlag, 1961)

Meyer, Michael R.: *A Handbook for the Humanistic Astrologer* (New York, Doubleday/Anchor Press, 1974)

Otto, W.F.: *The Homeric Gods* (London: Thames and Hudson, 1954)

— *Dionysus, Myth and Cult* (Bloomington & London: Indiana University Press, 1965)

Perera, Sylvia B.: *The Scapegoat Complex* (Toronto: Inner City Books, 1986)

Pierrakos, John: *Core Energetics* (New York: Life Rhythm Publications, 1987)

Spier, J.: *The Hands of Children: an Introduction to Psycho-Chirology*, (London: Routledge & Kegan Paul, 1944)

Stone, Hal & Winkelman, Sidra: *Embracing Our Selves* (California: Debross & Co, 1985)

— *Embracing Each Other* (San Rafael, California: New World Library, 1989)

Talking with Angels, a document transcribed by Gitta Mallasz (Einsiedeln: Daimon Verlag, 1988)

Wolff, Charlotte: *The Human Hand* (London: Methuen 1942)

— *The Hand in Psychological Diagnosis* (New York: Philosophical Library, 1952)

Index

RECENT TITLES FROM **DAIMON**:

Verena Kast
A TIME TO MOURN
Growing through the Grief Process

160 pages, paper
ISBN 3-85630-509-2

In perhaps her most important book, Verena Kast explains the role of mourning in the therapeutic process. Working as a psychotherapist, th author has often observed depressive illnesses caused by painful losses which have not been adequately mourned. Traditionally, mourning has not been a subject of psychologist attention. Verena Kast uses dreams to illustrate the stages of mourning and shows systematically how the unconscious stimulates us to encounter our grief.

Susan Bach
LIFE PAINTS ITS OWN SPAN
On the Significance of Spontaneous Paintings by Severely Ill Children

with over 200 color illustrations

Part I (Text): 208 pgs.,
Part II (Pictures): 56 pgs., 240 x 200 mm
ISBN 3-85630-516-5

Life Paints its own Span with over 200 color reproductions is a comprehensive exposition of Susan Bach's original approach to the physical and psychospiritual evaluation of spontaneous paintings and drawings by severely ill patients. At the same time, this work is a moving record of Susan Bach's own journey of discovery.